WEEK OF FIRE

by EARNEST LARSEN

Published by Pastoral Educational Services
Special Projects Division of
Paulist Press
400 Sette Drive, Paramus, New Jersey 07652

President: Rev. Kevin A. Lynch, C.S.P.
Vice President and Project Director:
Rev. Thomas E. Comber, C.S.P.

Editor and Photographic Selection: Joseph W. Nash
Production Assistant: Miss Rae Fronzaglia

Design: Ron Cutro Associates, Tenafly, N. J.

Picture Credits:
Lou Niznik—Pages: 6, 21, 23, 24, 31, 32/33, 35, 44, 55, 57, 75, 82/83
Peter Lange—Cover and Pages: 61, 66, 80
Sister Diane Smith—End Sheet and Pages: 3, 58, 72/73
George and Richard Egley—Pages: 8/9, 18/19, 78/79, 87
Ed Lettau—Pages: 11, 16/17, 37, 42
Joseph Foley—Page: 12/13
Donald Abram—Page: 15
Alan Mercer—Pages: 7, 26/27, 50/51, 70/71, 76/77, 88
Harry Sadel—Pages: 28/29
Robert Hollis—Pages: 40/41
Charles O'Connor—Page: 38
Alan Arluke—Pages: 48/49, 53, 62/63, 64/65
Thomas Connellan—Pages: 68/69
Arnold Arluke—Pages: 46/47
Thomas Lanno—Page: 85
(Black Star):
    Dan McCoy—Page: 92
    Richard Lawrence Stack—Pages: 90/91

Library of Congress
Catalog Card Number: 72-93751

ISBN O-8091-8755-8

Color Separations by:
Color Control Corp., Little Ferry, N. J.

Printed and bound in the
United States of America by:
R. R. Donnelly & Sons Co., Chicago, Ill.
G.T.O. Lithographers, Inc., Little Ferry, N. J.

This book is for CeCe

Contents

Emmaus Bound

Sometimes in thinking of Christ, strange scenes come to mind. Far from the omnipotent Lord of heaven and earth, the immensely pathetic image of a majestic caged eagle flashes before my mind's eye. Or I think of a mighty whale penned in a puny aquarium, or people stacked 80 stories high in towering apartments.

Eagles were not made to live in cages, nor whales to be the slaves of tiny tanks. People were not meant to subsist ant-like in concrete hives. And so with Jesus, the Word who came to move among his people, to break their bread with them and weep their tears. Often, like an outcast, we drive him into the wasteland of mere theory, or worse yet, transform him into some sterile statue even while he strains to embrace the very core of our lives.

Repeatedly we cry out in desperation, "Jesus where are you?" Then proceed to seek the God of life in realms other than life itself. Often, as some genie, we attempt to summon him from the cask of intellectual speculation. We act as if theorizing is synonymous with loving communication. Whereas in truth every day we travel the road to Emmaus with the mysterious Stranger falling exactly into step. To our companions we speak of many things: of God and hope, of death and the promise of resurrection. All the while the Stranger wordlessly repeats over and over,

"But I am with you. Look to your own lives for my presence. There you will find me. I am with you."

We continue to walk away from Jerusalem bewailing the fact that Jesus has died. All the while the Stranger keeps step waiting for us to break the bread of our own lives' experiences with him that the scales may fall and our eyes recognize who has been with us all the time.

What if the standard religious terms that often seem so boring were not abstract theological concepts at all? What if they were more than anything descriptions of God taking his place in the midst of our human experiences? Which is to say, in the midst of our own lives. Perhaps the Stranger is telling we Emmaus bound, blind pilgrims—would you understand my Calvary, then consider your own tears. For in that agony and only there can I take my stand in your flesh-and-blood world. *My crucifixion is not a page in a book, it is an event that has not stopped happening since I took you for my own.* Understand the agony of the alcoholic who, in desperation, shot himself to death before his wife and children. There I hang in all truth. Do you see that poor drunken Indian doing his war dance before the group of laughing youth on your downtown streets? Trading his heritage for a few quarters. If you cannot find the hill named Calvary there,

then you shall never find it. There is an eighth grade girl in your town; she is selling narcotics to her classmates. One of them went deaf due to her traffic.

My cross is also your frustration, your loneliness, your failure. Your guilt and shame which falls like rain in your inner self is the heart and soul of my cross. I am within you as you are within me.

It is there as well that you will find my resurrection. Why reduce this continuing victory to a matter of new hats and white flowers. How terribly we both diminish in such a petrification. Would you know the meaning of death—dying to life, then seek it where life holds its court. Look deeply into the magnificent eyes of the young handicapped girl who shall never walk again, yet has retained her lust for life. She tells all who listen, "I love life. I want to live every moment to the full." And she does. My resurrection is the policeman retaining his willingness to serve in kindness, even though he has been severely wounded in the line of duty; the teen-age boys working for pennies in a general hospital to bring joy to those no one else has time for. If you would place flowers before the empty cave of death let it be these. Living flowers with faces, hands and arms busy about the task of bringing life out of death. I have risen from the dead in you. Find me there or, for you, it has never happened. The meaning of my coming to life is that you, too, in my power, will embrace life with such gusto that death will fall before you. Find it in that arena or find it not.

Countless times we have broken bread together. Have you tasted me? Have you found me in your embrace of the Eucharist? Look, do you see how dark it is in the room of those two ancient ladies living out the end of their days in the rest home. The night to them is a foretaste of death; they are frightened and alone. Quietly, silently, do you see the chalk-white hands search out each other from between the beds. They meet. Do you see how they join, praying through the long hours. In truth they have found the meaning of my bread. Where charity and love prevail —there I am in the midst of them.

The poverty-stricken black minister and his community who shared what meager possessions they had with their sister recently released from the mental hospital; that is Eucharist. There I am.

All the lovely books that define, parse, historically trace the development of my body-sharing through the ages cannot substitute one second for a love-filled action of one of mine towards another. Such as the second when a man, standing solitary and brave before all the monumental death in this world, offers a frightened child the only thing that could possibly make a difference to him, "Trust me. I will not hurt you. Trust me." If he accepts that trust he will know the meaning of my Eucharist.

The New Fire you celebrate on the eve of Easter is not a sterile candle burning in a darkened building you call a Church. It is a mighty God-born hope, a hope deeper and greater than any fear that life can produce. I would send my New Fire rolling over the face of your earth if you would but have it. Just as I would send it flooding the domain of your consciousness if you would accept me. New Fire is the power of joy, often tested, as it rises above the reasons for despair. It can happen if you but believe. If you would but accept that I am in your midst, living my existence in the experiences of your life. Your homes can be centers of peace, your marriages a continually growing twining of lives, your hearts perpetually deepening altars of my daily sacrifice to the living God.

The project girl hungering for love, the settlement house manager who will not give up, the millions who dare risk, inch by inch, to reach toward spiritual progress—all are monuments to the power of my Fire. The New Fire that will and can renew this earth we both inhabit. It can, if you will but find me. And to find me you must find yourself as I find myself in your neighbor— for there I have written my name among men.

If we are to find the Living God among the land of the living, we must look where he passed. Not simply in this event or that happening, but in the process whereby he went from the ordeal of death to the victory of life. The summary of all Christian living is in the passage of Calvary to the Resurrection. Each year as the week of New Fire, Holy Week, comes and goes, we are invited to enter again into not only the historical events of Jesus' life but in our own identification with the Son of Man. Grasp its meaning now, and when it comes, its meaning will explode anew in you!

The limit of this identification is contingent only upon our own depth of faith, our own ability to see. Not a day passes that we do not take our stand in the midst of this deepest of all human dramas: the struggle against death in all its forms.

In our blindness we complain of boredom, lacking of "things to do." We say, "nothing ever happens," while all around us the hammer of Calvary beats out its dreadful hymn and the angels sing their joyful Alleluia as Christ shakes death from his feet. It is happening all around us, in every person we meet, in the innermost sanctuary of our own beings. We have but to see it, to reach out, to make it part of our daily existence. To see is to be absorbed; to participate in the adventure is to become holy.

Holy Week is not so only because it was of Jesus, but also because it is of us. It is our week as well. A week that speaks of a process, a journey, that stretches all the way to the shadow of our grave, a week *that takes place many times over each day* as we decide whether the process of conquering death will be ours or not. This very day is Holy Thursday and Good Friday, for this day we have been asked many times to share the Body of Christ; this day, perhaps hourly, we have been asked to climb the Hill of Skulls as Our Lord has before us. Easter is far more than an empty tomb on the hill outside Jerusalem; it is the empty tomb of fear and hurt of those all around; it is the putting aside of death of those near and dear to us whom we have enabled to rise. This day is Thursday and Friday and Saturday, this day is the day of the Rising of the Lord and the coming of the Spirit. The time is now, the person is you, the Power is God.

The trail has been opened, the journey has begun:

Monday through Wednesday
—Prelude To Vision

"LET HIM WHO HAS EYES TO SEE, SEE
LET HIM WHO HAS EARS TO HEAR, HEAR"

Every year Monday through Wednesday of Holy Week is the same. As if responding to some strange inner clock, all involvements, activities, frantic rushing about, stop. Life stands still to be inspected within the context of the Lord's dying and rising. Slowly, mercilessly, the light illuminates each particle of life asking, "What is going on here? What is happening?"

The first days of the Week of Fire are like an immense rally or convention held in the court of my own head. The experiences, thoughts, joys and suffering from the past year come home. They come back either dancing, or trudge in halt, lame and weary, wearing the indelible imprint of many people who have given them shape. In some strange, deeper than conscious, way they all find a new or deeper meaning in the happening called Easter.

As before, the parade of faces, voices, eyes is sweeping past. It was so while staring out on a beautiful lake in Wisconsin, while sitting on a bench in a little bum's park in St. Louis, or walking the streets of Chicago. Whenever this Monday dawns the strange homecoming begins. Now I sit in a small chapel in Minnesota while the snow softly swirls around the building. It has begun.

I hear again the sickening yelp of the poor deaf-mute woman who has her purse snatched late one night, the inexpressible misery in my mother's voice as she informed me my brother was a wounded Viet Nam statistic, the sledge-hammer effect of watching a liberated long-haired, head-banded youth on crutches and withered legs scurry across a Dallas street with his pals. Easter, perhaps, is mostly the ability to carry on, to care.

But there is also music. Slowly, with the sweetest tones, I feel in my hand the fingers of a teenage girl who has never reached out in her life. I see LaVern's glowing eyes as she reports her husband will not die of the cancer in his body. I smell the delicious presence of God in 83-year-old Olive's freshly baked bread.

What we are rushing toward is Easter—the ability to carry on with even fewer props and more reliance upon the Higher Power who is God. When will we learn that Jesus is not a fad, slogan or trip. That he really lived, really died and truly rose. And so do I.

14

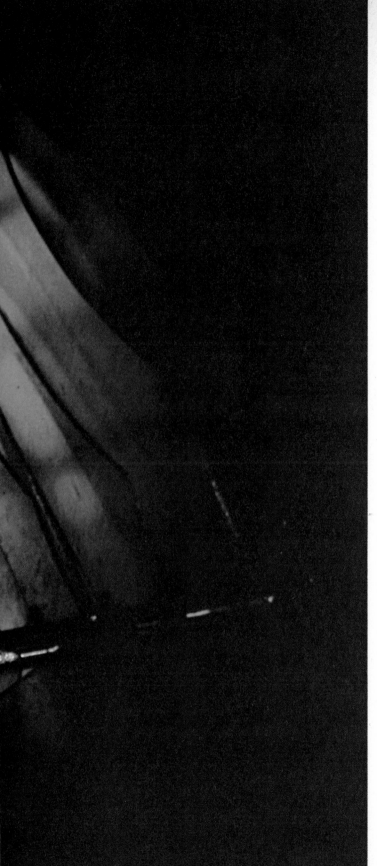

Who are you, Jesus?

In the first row at services sits an 18-year-old pill head. His mind slowly simmers and if the speed doesn't slow, will soon burn out. How he struggles through. I don't think he wants to die.

Behind his head of long curly hair sits a bald fireman. His service record is years long and so is the memory of abuse, danger and injury, not only from the fires but from those who hound the fireman. He has much hate and not a little amount of reason.

I saw Pat there—married to an on-again, off-again husband who is presently "off-again" the booze. Is he going to make it this time? Has he had a spiritual awakening?

Bill is also there. His mother is dying and all he can do is sit by and watch.

A tiny baby rests in the arms of his mother. See her face. She is God, viewing the first day of creation.

Someone prays for Al who is doing time in the state penitentiary.

Brian prays for his fifth grade classmate who desperately wants a bike.

Mike is next to him. He is afraid to speak. He desperately wants more desperate things.

The name on my bracelet says "Sgt. Peter Drabic—9/24/68." A POW since 1968.

This living book reads on in unending torrents. All breaking the bread who is Jesus.

Who are you, Jesus? Must we not look at your image rooted in all the mirrors standing about you? You told Philip he would see the Father if he saw you. But mustn't we see Philip as well to see you?

The early brothers prayed, "Maranatha"—Come Lord Jesus. And you have, so grandly and in such diverse forms, you have.

17

Behind our curtain, from the other side, what does it look like? Lord, I would try to break through the apparent, but false, surface scales that cover my eyes. Everything seems so routine, so ordinary. My desk is as I left it yesterday, the noises are the same, the work is old before it is new. How blind, Lord, how blind in your Temple.

I would throw my mind wildly into your infinity—I would be aware, to my so-limited capacity, of what you are moving and bringing to life everywhere. I am conscious that even though I *feel* no movement or sense of becoming, that your universe is in terrific motion, is always progressing. What is happening to us, Lord? Men tell me at some primal focus of existence, when matter existed in some congealed form, there was what (for lack of a word to describe a reality our minds cannot conceive) we call an explosion. From that point on, fragments have been hurtling out through space. But where are we now? We know the universe is expanding—still pushing out. We do not know if a gravitational break will, in some eon, slow down our expanding acceleration so that one "day" it may all converge back upon itself and start its process again.

Will we forever expand? What lies behind our shabby curtain of opaque blindness? Is "space" relatively infinite? We know so little. Man is an infant. I know, Lord, we neither know the secret of gravity, nor the true basic structure of earth's building blocks—the atom. We do not know the secret of light, energy, or even a fraction of the mystery of our oceans. As of yet, the study of the mind and its workings, of parapsychology, genetics and memory are at infant stages. And, Lord, no one even will be but a beginner at understanding what has happened by reason of your Incarnation.

I sit before so many open doors behind which is darkness—yet thrilled because I know they *are*. Mystified by the infinitesimal—the atom; by the personal—a smile, a tear; by the divine— "Abide in Me"; by the too-immense—a universe in motion.

We are not where we have been, or ever will be again. So many, many things, Lord, we can in truthful honesty only say, "what we call . . . ,"

for we can see them only in so narrow and limited a way: time, space, movement, reality—even (maybe especially) love. And a person could become lost; he could ask in despair—what is stable? Are there no roots? But this is the most beautiful of all chapters in your dialogue with men—what is stable, what is sure, is your love for us.

If you did not humble, stupify and dwarf man in the presence of your majesty, we would never find you. You are the God of the Weak.

᠁᠁᠁᠁᠁

The museum offered a mummy to look at. A large card standing beside his new pyramid of glass in the 20th Century said he was a priest of the god Hotep, a divinity worshipped when the Israelites were slaves in Egypt. It even said the golden calf made by the Israelites in the desert was probably after the image of Hotep. And this leathery, beetle-brown, tiny man stares up at me through empty sockets from centuries ago, inviting countless questions.

Hotep's servant has very high cheekbones and thin lips. Through various skull apertures you can almost peer into his brain cavity. I mightily wonder what thoughts coursed through that now-disintegrated brain.

What, little reverend of 4,000 years ago, did you believe? Were there stupendous wonders being constructed in your lifetime? Was there political unrest, and how magnificent was the court of Pharaoh? What did those empty eyes see of the Nile and the beauty of ancient Egypt?

I wonder if you knew Moses? That upstart leader of slaves who seems to have brought such havoc to your great nation. What did you think of their ridiculous allegiance to one God? Did that infuriate your master? But then what did you think when your army and Pharaoh did not return from their slave scavenger hunt? How fine and straight your nose, so delicate your hands. Did you wring them in misery when your first-born died of the strange illness? Or did you ever have a family?

How silent you are in your strange glass tomb while we unknowingly, unseeingly, glide by. I wish the empty holes of your eyes would fill and blink to life. Would you think our era was more civilized than your own, or less? Would you find us more or less refined? What would you think of these descendants of stammering Moses and his fickle clan? Could you believe the immense structures and number of followers of this one jealous God? How strange things would seem. All the while I look into your bony, petrified face I feel you, too, are watching me. Does your spirit hover over us? Two young girls just passed. They looked at you and moaned, "Oh, ish." Do you laugh at their blindness as they recoil from yours?

᠁᠁᠁᠁᠁

Is it not true to say: you see what you are prepared to see, hear what you are prepared to hear, experience what your capacities are receptive to. *A man lives only to the extent that he is prepared to live.*

My God, what a terrifying thought.

How little I am prepared. It is only ten a.m., an ordinary a.m. So much has come before me, so much slipped by. Ragged little Snooks was crying, carrying a problem that was so heavy. I couldn't shake it from him. Those sad, red eyes rimmed with tears. Did I really see? Or understand? How much more was there?

Sunshine breezed into school shouting, "Peace." All light, all smiles. I hardly noticed her.

There stands Angie, who has fallen again and is afraid to try over.

And Veronica, who deliberately crucifies her mother and hates herself for it. But, "I don't care, I hate her and she hates me."

Mark ran over between classes, like a boxer, shouting, "Come on, let's go a few rounds."

The whole schoolyard was full of kids jumping rope on the blacktop pavement. And it's only ten a.m. How much was there I didn't see? How many wordless messages went out I didn't see? What were you trying to tell me in the few hours I've been up this day, Lord?

᠁᠁᠁᠁᠁

I recall as a child often playing night games around a safe, mellow glow of a corner street light. It was not then the harsh brilliance of a

mercury vapor lamp that is so rude to night. The darkness of that decade was merely interrupted by courteous, soft electric bulb light. Perhaps the night was not as violent then. At any rate, all games revolved around the light as spinning planets around our sun. Often the curiosity of standing but a few feet outside the sphere of light and thereby becoming part of the night things, struck me. The light only went so far. Inch by inch one traveled to the edge—then darkness.

The street lamp has changed. Games have deepened to harsh reality, yet the psychic geography remains. Mankind acts out its history only within the confines of such a dim light casting such a faint "safe" glow. Inch by inch the braver of the species toe the edge of that rim of light looking hesitantly, anxiously out into the unknown. Will there ever be a time when, as a child, the proportions of darkness to street lamp will change?

This hour I sit looking awe-filled out onto the expanse of Lake Superior. A stone's throw away rushes a frothing river some say once was laden with fish. This is an old Indian portage. In some not too-distant past small campfires glowed here as men, quiet and lean as the forest, cooked their fish and tended their canoes. How wide they must have thought their circle of brilliance.

Perhaps, expanding the night darkness of their ancestors, they had found a better way to hunt the caribou, hook the trout, or trap the fox. Perhaps the camp of ghosts sitting so near are speaking of the new inventions brought by the French—of such "civilized" objects as guns, liquor and bounty paid for enemy scalps. For good or evil, the edge of light expanded. Man knew more. His consciousness of the familiar included knowledge undreamed of by their fathers.

How short a time has brought paved roads shooting into Canada and strange machines that would have scared our ghost ancestors beyond recall were they to look up the embankment and see one sail along, headlight eyes burning brightly, at seventy miles an hour. Tomorrow's ghosts familiarly speak of planet probes, Dow Jones industrial averages, summit meetings. Ah, but we are different. Just as the caribou hunters before us were different. And their fathers before them. "We" are not confined by narrow night lights sending our visionaries out to do battle with darkness. Not us! We, at last, are children of the light. We are on the verge of destroying darkness.

Up the beach just a bit burns another phantom fire. Around it sit the ghosts we will sire. What is their conversation? In what yet-to-be revealed magic do they traffic? Will they think they are more than children playing within the safe ring of a tiny flickering bulb?

Several hours ago I saw a man catch a big trout on a piece of yellow yarn. 300 years ago, the phantom men to my left probably used a bait of yellow feather. Maybe we haven't pushed the circle out as far as we think.

We stand, however, within the confines of our knowledge—light—not just as a race of living beings but as individuals. Collectively, it is thrilling to see "mankind" struggle against his limitations. There is strength in numbers. Alone, however, this same struggle is often terrifying.

Recently, a story was told of a young doctor who bucked the company in a town it owned. He had little to gain, everything to lose. The company wasn't hurting him. He had no reason to fight it, expose it. "Principle" was the reason he gave. This man stood at the rim of his light anxiously wondering how far he could extend it. Every ounce of moral courage welling within would be tapped. He would know who he was.

How few such men are. Far more often a man silently turns his back on the quest for expansion and never faces his unrevealed greater self. In failing to face the unknown, he becomes its victim.

I think we are not one large river flowing endlessly to the sea. Rather, we are innumerable drops that can be viewed separately. In fact, must be viewed so, if we are to grasp the whole. Each individual toeing the edge of his fears, peering out beyond the night of his own personal limitations. Each one wrestling with the question of whether or not to silently steal beyond his own safe circle.

Funny about crying. All you can say for sure is that a person crying feels something awfully deep.

Huge gentle tears ran over Sue's eyes. Actually, it was about Larry and someone being good to her most unexpectedly. Larry said, though poor, they had a fantastic marriage. In fact, "We have been so low we rationed out potato chips between us so the kids could eat. Like right now, we have five cents till Thursday to live on."

Larry was very serious about getting his head screwed on tightly. He is trying hard to clear away the rubble so he can find his God. Sue was so happy about this. But the tears came when a friend, who had no particular reason to care, except that he was a friend, slipped her some money.

Tom's dad cried because his son had shot himself to death.

Alice cried because she felt the experience of love so deeply.

Jeannie cried because she had to leave her volunteer job at the state mental hospital at summer's end. How painfully she would miss the people she cared for in the blind ward: Michael, with such withered eye sockets, who pirouetted on his toes all day to music only he heard. Lee, who violently clapped his hands to Johnny Cash's music and loved to sing, ". . . smoking big cigars." Perhaps, most of all, Charlie, who was part Mongoloid, and had the neatest way of saying, "Yahhh, gimmee pop, yahhh." How she would miss them.

When Jeannie got home, her little sister was crying because her brother had hit her with a toy truck and her mom cried with happiness because she was back home.

Funny about crying.

ഗഗഗഗഗ

This room is semi-dark. Whirring motors from the cooling system quietly chase each other. Every so often other motors from various machinery kick in. It will be dawn soon but no one will see it. The thick rain clouds are grey and heavy. What kind of a day will it be?

A day of concern. Dave McMillen with his crippled arms folded tightly together and his jerky head lying on his pillow had managed to tell his grandmother, "I hope you are better tomorrow." She had a cold. Dave had a temperature of 104 and was flirting with pneumonia. But he didn't hurt so much he couldn't laugh. For how many will it be that kind of a day? Filled with heroic concern.

A day of misery. Angela had an abortion. She is only 18. How badly she wanted the baby. She and Richard were going to get married. But no, her parents couldn't stand the shame and disgrace of the growing time. They were money people and had enough to take care of this "problem." They did. Yet they created a new one. Angela is blowing up from the inside out. She cries all the time, can't sleep, can't concentrate. Guilt mixed with fear and self-hatred surrounds her every second. How many will drag these same elements of misery through every moment?

Nice day. Cindy can't wait to get her camper-trailer and get going. She is going to visit British Columbia, Michigan, and God-knows-where. "Let's get it on," she says.

A day of wanting. Andy sits all alone in the old folks' home. He talks forever about getting home—back to his flowers, berries and birds. I wonder if he will ever make it. On his wall hangs a picture of a horse a five-year-old drew for him. He says it's a horse, anyway. Andy has lots of drawings like that.

How many others—how many different situations. The sky is lighter now. Day will happen all right.

But what kind of day will it be? It will be a Jesus-day. One filled with dying and rising, with searching and reaching out. It will be a day when I will be asked to die a little that I might rise with the Lord. What more could one ask than to take his place in this drama that alone is the meaning of human life.

Yes, truly, again as every day, it will be a Jesus-day.

ഗഗഗഗഗ

Last two hours of school. So much is going on, so much already just memories. The ice cream man stopped at the pit across the street to sell to the construction workers. A white guy was by the wagon and hollers down to his black buddy, "Hey, man, whadda ya want." Last night at our closing banquet everyone was in rare form, happy, celebrating. All through the meal one of the teachers waltzed around pouring wine into crystal glasses perched on the immaculate white tablecloth. A big candle on each table glowed, saying, "All is cool." And coffee . . . black girls floated in and out. "Would you like coffee?" " Can I pour you some coffee?" Smiles and polite as could be. But on the sleeve of one smiling girl, little but not too little, were two words, "Black Power." I wonder if behind the smile she was pouring poison into every cup.

Simon and Garfunkel turned the whole civic auditorium on. Songs about equality and illusion, about reality and truth. Everyone clapped, stomped and went home. On the El coming back, I was across from a very uncivilized-looking black man—fat, hat turned up, thick glasses. Next to him was his "woman." No teeth, chewing tobacco, sweating up a storm. She held a beautiful little girl on her lap. The man and woman were tenderly holding hands. You tell 'em, Simon and Garfunkel.

That El—what fantastic books could be written about the El. Trains screech around corners so close to tenement buildings they take the brick dust with them. It's kind of like watching an old movie where you insert a nickel and watch through a scope. In split-second flashes, you witness people eating, sleeping, relaxing; people fighting, laughing and loving. Only it isn't a movie and the camera is you. Privacy becomes a luxury that, not existing, has no real meaning. The noise of the iron intruder has become so integrated with "me-now," that it doesn't exist. On one of these runs, I saw a man painting his window frames in a space so small he could hardly get between the house and the El tracks. I wonder what name they would give this action in psych class, "self-actualization by efforts to improve the climate of the environment." Maybe that's it.

The people who ride the El are fascinating beyond all description. The glassy-eyed and knife-eyed, the sleepy-eyed and eyes with excitement burning in them, the insolent and totally dependent, the unconcerned and the hostile. All thrown together for forty cents in a cheap brotherhood of going someplace else. Every time a person runs in the car for fear of having the door slam on him, a new mystery enters your life.

The lake should be another book. The huge, majestic, wise lake. A million years ago, as now, it rolled in on the beach. As now, it saw primitive men love and murder. Before people wore clothes, in their simplicity they watched the lake. Now in their sophistication, they hardly wear any and still look at it thinking the same thoughts. Neptune must enjoy men. A thousand years from now perhaps man will be simple again—but he will think the same thoughts and be touched by the same sense of "greater than I exists" as he watches the rolling waves. The little kids who see nothing but their world, their sand and bugs and paper cups to play with; their mothers who see nothing but them and watch for their safety; the countless beautiful girls *so* anxious to show

the world what they have grown to, so anxious to be seen and accepted, yet so coy, feigning insult at the recognition they court. An eternal game. Man, the eternal actor.

Early in the morning there is a very thin bronze young woman in a bikini who runs the length of the beach next to the water. Not fast, but very controlled, straight and dignified. She is very, very beautiful, running. I wonder if McLuhan's predictions about sex in the future aren't correct. 100 per cent correct. All of life is more sensual, sex is spelled with a small "s." It's no big deal, simply an integrated part of the whole spectrum. At any given time of day or night, you see people "making love." Making something. Often making shame and guilt which gets little press. In a storeway in the heart of the loop, hands fly, every tree in every park has looked down on a blanket love scene, and the beach is a continual mating ground. No one cares especially. If it's time, well, it's just time, like time to eat and time when I'm so tired I can't keep my eyes open. And if it isn't time, fine. Maybe tonight or tomorrow. The contradiction is kind of sad. The whole "personalization set" takes away the individuality of the body. Then how are you different than me? We are all persons—but all the same. "Baby, you got nothing new." True. But *she is* new. And yet, it is a scream to pass a bench on which old ladies are perched like birds on a telephone line watching all the body-giving. What memories bring yesterday back to you? And love, to whatever degree it exists, the young couples will always be beautiful. Here is another book. The misty and mysterious surface of young couples walking together. Pass by and you can feel the sensation, sense the flow. Saying something in a laugh or silence—speaking constantly: we are together.

⁓⁓⁓⁓⁓⁓

Joe's human world is packed, sardine-close, with every conceivable contrast. Standing side by side are those who absolutely cannot show affection and those who have to grab everybody that comes within arm's length. Both sick about the same thing, yet one stands at the front door and one at the back. There are the wise and those who think they are, the happy and those who wish they were, the gentle and those who cannot be, the givers and the takers. Maybe most striking is unseeing innocence, eyeball-to-eyeball with pitiful human failure . . . like Joe. Like you and me. Like Jesse.

Jesse is seven. His pal Andy is the same. We were all messing around—Jesse pulled my coat and wanted to know if he had an orange ring around his mouth from his soda. Andy and I said, "Yup—it goes all the way from your chin to your forehead." Which it did.

Then seven-year-old Jesse told us about the divorce. There was so much fighting at home, his parents decided to call it off. "It's going to be in June," he said.

Andy's face showed growing excitement. "No kidding. Is it going to be June 7?"

Jes said, "Yeah, I think it is." He would have said yes to June 35th!

"Good deal," shouted Andy, "that's my birthday!"

Yeah—real good deal.

⁓⁓⁓⁓⁓⁓

All the kids came marching up on the stage singing, "Open the door, come on in, I'm so glad to see you, my friend." All such nice-looking kids. A couple behind me said, "Those aren't the troublemakers. The only ones you hear about are the dope addicts, troublemakers. Those are good kids."

Maybe. But why does everything have to be so absolute? What an intolerable burden we place on anyone when we expect them to be all good or all bad. No one is either. The sparkling clean faces on the stage aren't all good, just as the dirtiest kid shooting dope in some raunchy alley isn't all bad.

There once was this woman, a horrible sinner, taken in adultery . . . they brought her to Jesus.

⁓⁓⁓⁓⁓⁓

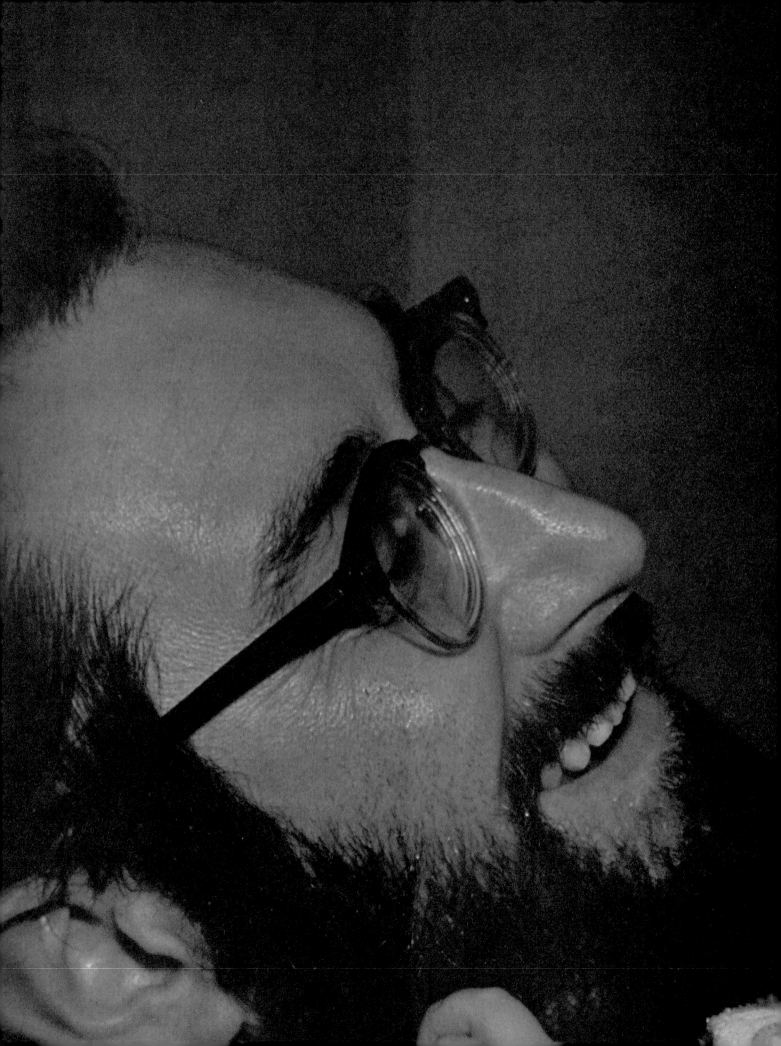

Thursday—Day of Love

"THIS IS MY BODY—THIS IS MY BLOOD
LOVE ONE ANOTHER"

If the world is flying apart in a million insane pieces, love is the only glue holding together whatever part is sticking whole. Only love allows a mad world to make sense.

Barb is no beauty. Except for her perpetually beaming face and the joyous sounds she makes, you would call her a vegetable. She can move no part of her body nor control any of her bodily functions. Put her in a car and she doesn't have the ability to sit up straight. Barb's eyes are continually in the process of closing and saliva always seems to fill her mouth. But beautiful! Ask Tommy. Tom loves her.

He arranged a fine supper at his house with his mother and sisters as cook and hostesses. The highlight of the evening was when he managed on his crippled legs to push Barb's chair over by the picture window all by himself. With the help of a friend he climbed aboard his huge three-wheel bike and headed outside. The street had a small incline running in front of the house sporting a thrilled girl sitting in the picture window. Tom came down that street like the king of all cycle riders. To Barb he was. And is.

All the way back to the home Tom and Barb kissed, yet never touched once. The light in their faces was radiant. Barb didn't have the power to even hold the beautiful bouquet of flowers Tom had his Mom buy. But she was holding something far more precious than that. Without love the world is insane for anyone.

Scott doesn't know much about the world. He is only four. Even at that age, he is blind and so hyper he is continually under heavy sedation. To make it strike three, he is living in an old folks' home. Why there, I don't know—but he is. Scott's parents love him dearly, but can't change what is. What magnificence in seeing the light in this blind child's face when he hears his parents' Thunderbird drive up. The sound of that car's engine is a beautiful word to him. It says, "I have brought someone you love and who loves you."

Maybe nothing can make sense of a blind four-year-old, hyper boy living in an old folks' home. But I know if love were not there, it would be tragic beyond any sense whatever.

And Louise loves her husband and son. Every time she even thinks of them, her eyes get misty. Her boy is a pillhead who is not going to stop using drugs for anyone. His father said, fine, but if you are going to live in this house you live by our rules. So the boy left. In this case, it appears absence makes the heart grow bitter. At least between father and son. Louise finds herself in the middle countless times. In the middle trying

to reconcile the warring parties; trying to see her boy without upsetting her husband—or simply wanting to talk about him; she is pulled apart when she attempts to speak to her son in favor of his father. Caught so many ways.

Love is glue that sometimes isn't strong enough. Yet love is all the world has going for it.

∽∽∽∽∽∽

To analyze a symbol is surely to destroy it. It is to make it incapable of saying the mystical, wonder-filled, human truths that try to speak through it. Truths like: I trust you, thank you, trust me, together we stand, I am sorry. How tragically we have done just that to the Eucharist.

I think of a man returning from war, stepping from the plane, embracing his wife and children. With every fibre of his being he is saying: I am with you. I have risked death and loss of you, but I am back with you now, and forever. Together we will face all the demons destined to rise before us and glory in facing a million times a million sunsets knowing that the day was ours for we had each other. This is presence.

What a ridiculous thing to envision the man stepping from the plane and find not greeting but question as to whether this is his body or blood, his spirit alone or spirit and body? To wonder what is the proper, the "right" way to accept this coming home? The man doesn't want a formal class on etiquette; he wants a loving welcome from his beloved. He wants his presence accepted for what it is.

How magnificent when Eucharist means this. What if it wasn't a theological speculation or Liturgical problem—let alone a source of disunity—but simply a loving statement from the heart of Christ—"Hey, I am here, with you." The world wouldn't know what to do with it. What if all of those who broke bread were saying: *Really,* you don't have to be afraid! What if every person who was ever baptized carried on them the outward sign of the ancient Hebrews of captivity: blood on the door post of their dwelling. And this sign said on the level of the symbol, the deepest of all human levels: No,

really, you don't have to be afraid, I am for you.

We are so afraid. Afraid of being alone and in a crowd; afraid to risk personal relationship and of being without it; afraid of failure and, mostly, unable to handle success; afraid to be really different and hugely afraid of being lost in the crowd; afraid to live and afraid to die.

But what if the Eucharist were the symbolic way for us to hear from God and say to each other: Do not be afraid. If you march to a mountaintop I am with you; if you enter shadows, I am right beside you; if it snows on your ship, then I will be cold too; and if the sun shines, then we both will bask in its warmth.

∽∽∽∽∽∽

I happened by noon services at a downtown church. Fifteen full minutes before its start the building began to fill. Where do all the ancient ladies come from? By service time, nearly 600 were there. The average age was at least 60, probably closer to 70. A strange phenomenon was taking place. Small pockets of cronies were sitting together. Periodically, a new old lady would trudge up the aisle to her accustomed place. She would be greeted by the warmest wrinkle-faced smiles of her pals. No doubt every noon the same little group formed. The greetings had all the feel and similarity of young athletes slapping each other's hands before a game, or loud boisterous shouts as men greet each other at a neighborhood bar. Belonging. Guaranteeing each other that they belong. Saying "this is our group."

Yet not the same. These ladies were not at a game or pub. They were at church, attending their God.

The service started. The atmosphere crackled with the anticipation of hundreds of old ladies waiting for the firm young hand of God to caress their souls.

∽∽∽∽∽∽

Why, oh why, can't we be gentle one to another! Meg is and smiles so beautifully. But she is tired and a little depressed. She asks in her unspoken voice, "Will you treat me gentle?"

Trish is worried over the operation she will have this summer. Due to its early date, she will have to take final exams early. Another worry. She is just kind of down. Who will treat her gentle—without sharpness or "that's your problem" attitude?

Bill, at immense inner cost, is singing with the church group. He is no ball of fire, but a young man brave enough to violently deal with his problem. He is just kind of there. Will anyone see? Or care? Or be gentle?

Mike is about the same. Only, at several years younger, he tries to become part of the group by being "cool." He talks too much and too loudly. He pushes in a very nagging kind of way. A gentle hand would do much to calm the terrifying storm.

Jean is coming out of the dark because another Mike has seen her. She is special to him. Therefore, to herself. A gentle touch.

The little group around me ten minutes ago was so totally "ordinary." That is, so greatly in need of gentleness. How the cycle goes round. Until you find it, you can scarcely give it. But until you are given the miracle spirit healer of gentleness by another, someone else's need is hardly paramount in your concern. Yet, if man does not begin to feed his brother the bread of life, are we not all condemned to die in our human wilderness?

Meg, feed Bill. Your concern would illuminate his soul like a volatile, Roman candle, million-mile-high sunspot eruption. And then Bill, your mission is to love Trish, who will accept Mike, who will then be able to . . .

I have recently discovered the word "hologram." A hologram is a complete unit, whose meaning is inherent in itself; it does not depend on relationships for its wholeness. A tree before a mirror is whole and entire. Break the mirror in a hundred pieces and you have not a fragmented tree but 100 whole and entire trees. Each piece contains its meaning within itself. No one piece is dependent on the remaining 99 for its wholeness. Is not each man, notwithstanding our many differences, a hologram of the human race. How like that mirror, broken or unbroken, we are.

Within each Meg, Trish, Bill or Mike is the totality of Man in microcosm. What is essentially true of one is true of all. Deny any the ark of love and his world is devastated. Take from any the gut level knowledge that he is precious and, as all holograms, you can safely say for all, he will not survive. A gentle touch is as essential to one, and therefore, all, as rain is to a waiting crop. If any one is mute in the way of expression of inner feelings, it is safe to say he is imprisoned in a most painful cell.

Yes, we are very different, as trees are different. Differing in climate adaptation, needle or leaf size, susceptibility to this or that disease. But all trees! Each a hologram of tree-ness unto itself.

Perhaps the words of Christ were spoken to Man the hologram—capable of considerable interpretation yet touching as direct as an arrow the truth that resides on the common level of man-as-hologram.

In John's gospel, Christ asks Peter three times, "Do you love me?" Each time Peter said, "Yes." Then why repeat three times?

Jesus asked his "Rock", "Do you 'agape' me?" "Agape" is the deepest form of love. Love that reaches out even when you may not feel whole yourself.

Peter responded, "Lord, you know I 'phillos' you." A word that represents a lesser degree of relationship. A giving to a point: a serving but only after I am safe; a reaching out, but not with the whole arm. Only the *third* time did Peter proclaim, "Lord, yes, I 'agape' you." Consequently, only then did Christ commission him to "feed his sheep." Only agape love will open the gate to that grazing land when it is the last stand of pasture remaining.

Few receive gentleness. Therefore, few give. Yet it is universally true in the case of one as in all that it is desperately needed. Who will begin?

Perhaps Christ knew this well. Maybe he knew all about holograms before the word was ever coined. Maybe that is why he pushed Peter to proclaim "agape" so that Meg would understand the meaning of this Day of Love.

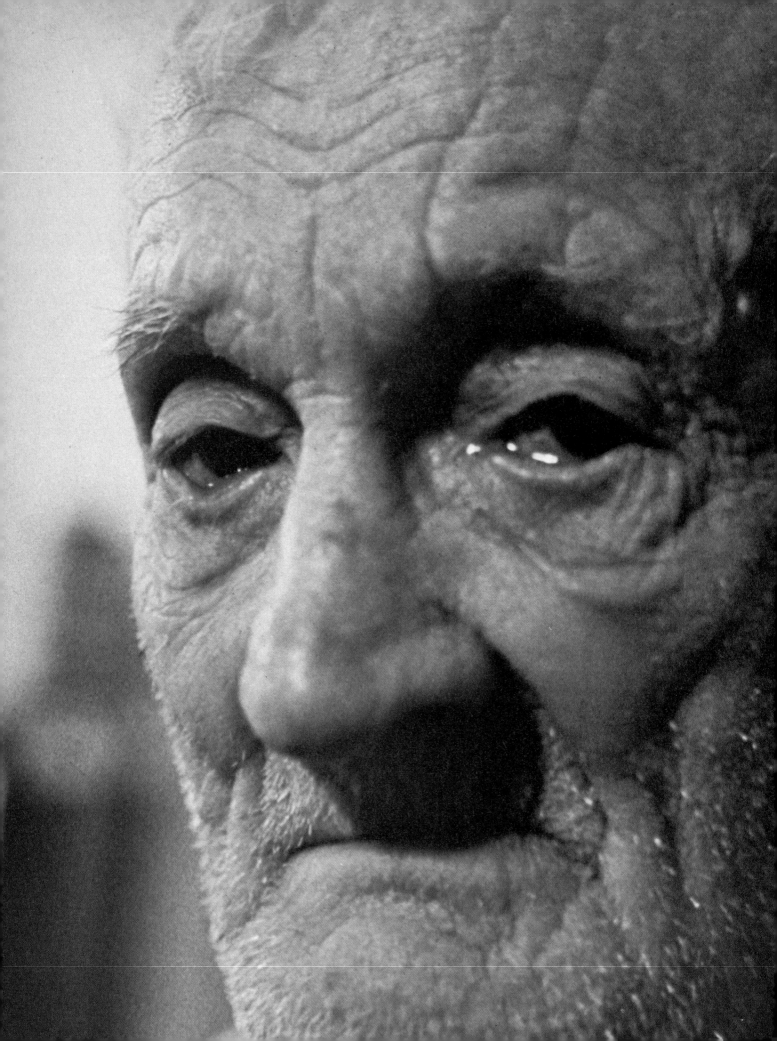

Jerry and Tom are great kids. Upon graduation they got jobs as orderlies at the General Hospital because they "believe in it." Jerry showed me an old man, Arthur, who got his head broken by a lead pipe when someone rolled him. The old man was full of bitterness and hatred. But Jerry wouldn't let him escape. He talked to him every day, joked with him, looked him in the eyes. The old man talks to people now. Someday he may not even hate. If he doesn't, that gift of life is from his young orderly.

But they both are quitting. Hitting the road during the summer. Next year maybe something else. Somehow it is a great pity. You believe in this, both of you; why not stick at it? Why something else? Why move on?

Suffering offends so many people, but not enough who will make relieving it their lifetime work. You are young though. Maybe you just have to try new sets of wings. Will you ever fly back to this? I hope so.

Jerry, one of Arthur's million-fold brothers is checking in one hour after you leave. Who will give him the gift of life? Who will break bread with him?

♒♒♒♒♒♒

Is it silly to say, "As your home goes, so goes the world?" Maybe not. If there is general blindness, general apathy, general selfishness riding over the earth like the dread horsemen of the

Apocalypse, is it not so because they are born, bred and boarded in our homes? Is it not folly to place impossible expectations on councils, assemblies and political parties when they can do no more than mold and re-mold the clay given them? If it be inferior, then what else the vessel they produce.

Brave new structures are not the total answer. There must be brave new people as well to operate those structures. Would that vast torrents of New Fire would leap upon our homes, would seize and totally engulf countless husbands and wives as they carry out their daily task of making the sun to rise. How hugely important for the universe that tenderness, no matter how young and weak its shoots, would begin to break through stony ground. Is it so impossible that the vision which allows spouses as people, let alone lovers, to see each other as people and lovers would dawn over the night mountains? Not objects, not obstacles to freedom, not competition or release valves—but lovers. Can that vision not happen? Is it possible that husbands and wives could talk? That lying side by side the words be but symbols inviting one another to truly care and share. What a glorious change would come over this world if there could be tears of delight instead of pain, touches of reverence instead of slaps, looks of consuming trust and sweetness rather than icy glares of suspicion.

Yet so many say it is impossible. The fire cannot enter. "You do not understand," they say. "Our marriage is old, blunted"; "we have seen too much of each other's weakness"; "the honeymoon is over"; "we have faced reality." As if death were the only reality. As if to understand meant only to surrender. Yes! The fire *can* enter. New life can begin. Death is *not* the only alternative. You need but to will it, to but open wide the door of your sanctuary and let the altar flame rage. It can happen.

But if you do, not only you will be reborn in the image of God, but the heavens as well will rejoice in your triumph, in the happiness that is yours in taking your place at the Banquet of the Lord.

It was late afternoon; I felt spent when the Negro minister entered. My first reaction was to disappear.

If any man looked like trouble, it was he. His little goatee was ragged, several of his teeth were missing. He wore brown pants and his black hat's broad brim was turned up. In some rummage store, no doubt, he had picked up a black clergy shirt, missing the white collar, however. With him was a tiny shrunken old lady with scar tissue surrounding her eyes. She looked like a boxer who never won a fight. Her hands constantly twitched, and her shoes didn't match. I'll never forget the faded pink dress she wore. It must have been the long-discarded favorite of some school girl. I came out to meet them thinking, "Dear God, what now?"

The man did indeed turn out to be a minister in some little sanctified religion around the corner. The woman had been a longtime patient of a mental hospital. The minister said, "Father, I am a parson. One of my congregation found this lady on the street; she just got out of the hospital and can't quite take care of herself yet. If she's alone she might kill herself.

"So me or one of my congregation is with her all day. We got her a little cold water flat and one of us is always with her.

"We share what pots and pans we got so she won't starve. But, Father, we don't have much food as it is—and we don't have none to give her. Could you possibly help us out so that at least we could get this lady somethin' to eat?"

There I stood—a Pharisee. How like the hypocrite at Simon's house, saying, "If only he knew what manner of woman this was, certainly he would not allow her to touch him." Christ was black in this case. He didn't care how desperate or shaken or beat up the little lady was—she was his sister. The congregation didn't care if they had only three or four pots between them, one was hers. The only thing they couldn't give her was what they didn't have: food. Concern they shared.

Thank you, Lord, for such giants to move among us.

"Trust." What magical description of God it is. Alone, really alone, is to live without trust. Bottled up, unknown, shadow-like in a world of flesh and blood. To live without trust is to live without hope; Dante's definition of hell. Discover the power to trust and you discover the power to live.

Even though every fibre of a person's being screams out the desire to trust, it resists actualization. Trust demands honesty, self-honesty, or there is no revelation. But it is exactly this terrifying, uncertain leap into the light of another's confidence that heals, restores, recreates. What I reveal under the banner of trust is me. But how shall I do this if I am a stranger to my own eye?

What an immense gift we ask of another when we say, "Trust me." Trust me with the truth that is yourself. Trust me with your dreams, that I will not ridicule them; with your inner thoughts, that I will reverence them; with your problems, that I will not insult you by making light of them; with your strength, that I will not diminish it; and mostly, with your weakness that I will not think less of you for it. Trust me with yourself, that in returning this gift, you may find you are more precious than ever you dreamed.

Yes, I know it is asking much of you. It is risky. But please take it. Give me your night and I will return to you your brightest noon. All I can ask is—trust me.

~~~~~~~~~~

About twenty teen-agers filled the room. Fantastic kids. Absolutely brimming over with energy, goodness, joy and beauty. It glowed in that room like a soft light around a burning match struck in the dark. But something else was there: fear and self-doubt. That filled the room, too, like torrid heat waves flooding from an open furnace door.

Uncertainty and blindness concerning self is all part of being young for most kids. But looking around, how unbelievable to realize these beauties really don't think much of themselves. Scores of adults I know would absolutely give *anything* to have the free glamour of youth, to be able to get genuinely high on nothing but soda

and each other. You are so rich. Don't be too long to grasp it.

Maybe especially you, Troika. Especially you, because I am thinking of you. One of you was afraid to shake the maracas while everyone sang. "I can't," you said. But you did. And your beautiful face beamed. Then the song ended. You stopped. Like an eclipse of the sun, you vanished. Your body was there, but you weren't. So often you only look down. Girl, look up. No one is over you with a whip! They stand before you destitute asking for your gifts. *You* are the giver. You are the only one who holds the whip. And you use it on yourself. Look up.

Even worse is you, the third member. As the saying goes, "I would tell you so much if you could hear it." You sat there so glum. Yes, you were tired, but also blue. "I can't sing, dance, draw or run," you say. "My sisters can, but I can't." Girl, open your eyes. Can't you see the world around you is a huge honey bee? Can't you really see how anxious they are to share of your beauty? To somehow touch it so they too may walk more fully in joy. You are so much a precious treasure. It seems impossible to believe you can't understand the power of your smile, the greatness of your presence.

Remember when a group of you picked me up late at night at the airport? I was so tired and empty I could hardly walk. Your huge smile and gentle being—these made me feel so good. Such a beautiful gift to have to give. I suspect you can sing and dance, draw and run much better than you think. But you are of so much more importance than that.

All of you are. Your magnificence is the best-kept secret in town. The sad part is the only one who doesn't know it is you.

~~~~~~~~~~

Both ladies were named Anna. One was three years younger, however, only 87. They shared a room in a rest home.

Young Anna's stroke left her without the ability to talk, walk and a completely paralyzed left side. She could sit in a wheel chair, however.

Her roommate could talk fine. But she could not sit in a chair. Her stroke left her right side unusable. Often, as is the case with the aged, night pounced upon them like an enemy bringing pain and fear.

There was a defense, however. Old Anna said, "Whenever we have pain, we reach out and hold hands. We pray together. That's the only way we get through some nights."

What power in two chalk-like, brittle hands slowly reaching out through bed guards in the night. As always, the defense of pain and loneliness is human touch. Even if you have but one hand with which to do it.

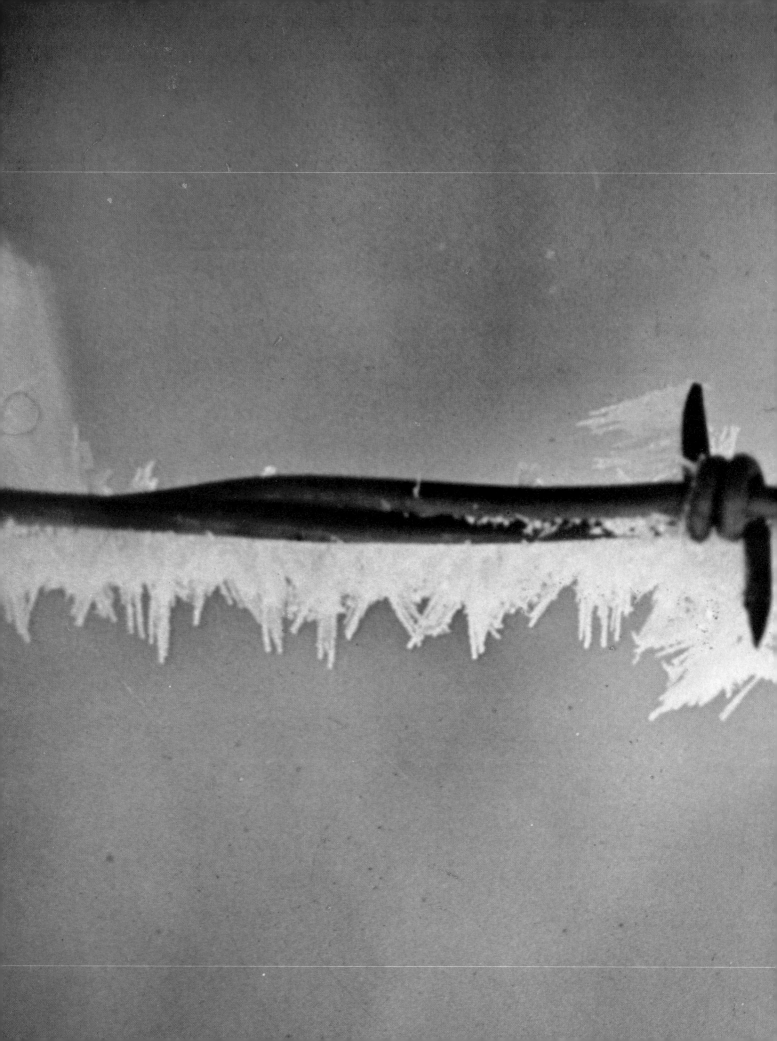

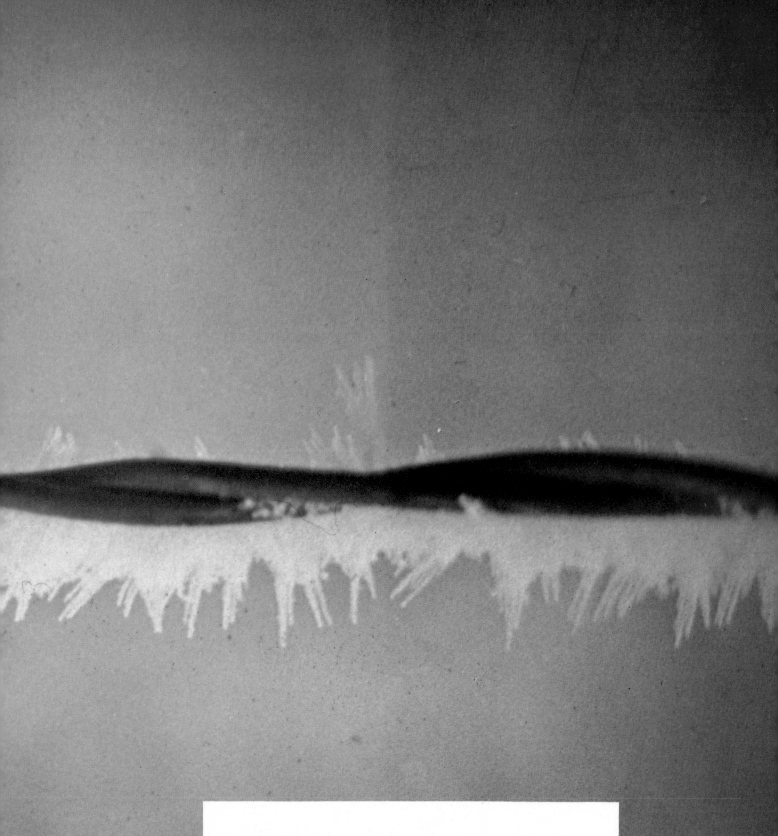

Friday—Day of the Cross

"HE TOOK THE VINEGAR BOWED HIS HEAD AND DIED"

Midnight—I walked the streets of downtown watching, feeling Christ live and die. A lovely, freckled-face girl about 17 or so with a long flowing blue coat, hustled by. It was very cold. Her eyes were so red and watery. What Calvary had she just come from? To what empty room, or house, or pair of arms, was she rushing? Would there be an Easter for her? Ever?

In a second she was gone. Hurrying by in the middle of the street going in the other direction. So badly I wanted to catch up to her. Say something, do something; give her something that would at least promise a dawn. But I turned around and she was gone. So helpless.

A person could board a plane and travel a million miles. Upon deplaning he would find the same demons he left waiting at the ramp. I have seen that same girl's face in countless cities, and will again. The same demon of loneliness and fear in all of them. Where have you gone, freckled-face girl? Where are you now?

Two blocks further, a well-dressed man stood jauntily by a parking meter outside a nightclub. A wide yellow tie flopped up and down on his blue shirt. Sophistication itself. Then he threw up like a waterfall. A derelict in a near-by doorway laughed wildly.

What does it all mean, Jesus? How does it all fit?

The old hunchbacked waitress at the greasy spoon asked her wino milk-drinking customer, "Is it this quiet in all the beer joints tonight?" I wonder if he could see out of his baggy eyes? He slowly moaned, "Yup." So she put money in the jukebox and played "Tell the Truth and Shame the Devil."

Three outlandishly dressed couples were laughing so hard coming out of the movie. Enjoying each other to the nth degree. When the light changed they all skipped across the street together.

Jesus is a sailor bouncing on the waves of fickle humanity.

Friday—He didn't quit. How he had reason to. But he didn't. Maybe more—he had the power to not only stop, but revenge the ignorance and injury heaped upon him by the pack of hounds dragging him down. That is the thing—he *could* have struck back and won. Yet he kept the proportions of the clown and carried on. How easy to intellectualize the crucifixion, to turn it into the smoke of theory when in reality it is the anchor of all our lives. The simple question of quitting or not.

Every time the crucifixion pricks my consciousness, I think of the old derelict walking into the shabby restaurant with clean shirt and tie. Faded, patched, worn, but clean. And a tie. Why should he continue the facade of dignity and respectability? Why can't he accept the fact that he just hasn't made it? All the other men around the stools have. His face is as worn as theirs, his situation as desperate or he wouldn't be here. Why pretend? That silly tie!

What a magnificent, great man he is.

Jung speaks often of archetypes. Feelings, drives, needs that are common to all of humanity. Symbolic types that both speak to and express what is all of us. Buckminster Fuller almost in the same way speaks of generalizations. That is, a philosophical or scientific truth that is sufficiently wide to admit of no exceptions. If there is an exception, it no longer is a general truth.

I wonder what both of these men would say of the Good Friday meaning?

An archetype deeper than all of humanity and a generalization of the greatest magnitude. Truly guilt and redemption are archetypes. But that God would die to give us life is "other than" humanity. It comes from outside the realm of our deepest inner self.

Wave after wave approached the cross and kissed it. Is it a generalization that, given the *proper circumstance,* all men would choose unity over chaos, good over evil, light over darkness? Black and white lips that speak only hatred touch the same spot. Is that not kissing each other? A teen-ager with a goatee and chain around his neck kisses the cross followed by an aged protector of the old order. Cultured ladies who abhor any hint of disease or dirt commonly embrace the Lord who holds lepers, derelicts and all manner of "fallen people."

Like a door opening and shutting. Only a second. But while it swings open no one minds the germs or who went before them or will follow. They all stand generally together within the deeper-than-man symbol of Christ.

Then the door closes and all withdraw and return to what often is an insane existence.

The Indian wasn't old. He didn't appear drunk. Yet on a downtown street he stopped a bunch of teen-agers and did a "war dance." Shuffling around with a huge paper-thin smile that seemed to say, "So what the hell, isn't this worth a quarter?" The kids nervously laughed and gave him coins. As soon as they had gone, his smile dissolved into inscrutable granite. What was going on behind his death mask smile? Only the wish to keep his boat afloat. As best he can.

Two other Indians, one drooling with eyes swollen almost shut, sat on a bench in the early morning sun. Their perch was in front of the library. By eleven they had moved. All the way to a second bench, for the morning sun had left the first bench in shadows. By six they had reached the last bench. Another day run its

course. Where would night find them? Call them what you will—how rough their sea. How frail their boat.

Inside the library a raggedy little man in a huge brown coat was telling two amazed pre-teens, "I've been around the world four times. I know all that's in these books." His twin brother, only older, taller, more gaunt, was eating a bowl of chili in a near-by mission. Tattooed on the first joint of each finger of his right hand: LOVE. And another very plain, overweight girl waited for a light to change so she could cross the street. My how mod her clothes! All the way to her smart beige leather cap. She looked ridiculous except for the fact that like the tattooed hand, and world traveler, and dancing Indian, she was simply trying desperately to keep her boat afloat.

No one wishes it to sink.

Have you seen Elie Wiesel on television? He has lived through more terror and suffering than most men can imagine or endure. Now there he is on television, narrating some footage of the Nazi nightmare he lived through. Among so many aspects of the concentration camp reality that is incomprehensible, is the fact, "that could be me!" The accident of birth in a different time and place and it would have been.

The old film footage showed soldiers armed with machine guns beating an old lady on the head with whips. Then they picked her up and threw her in a truck. That could have been my grandmother. But for the chance accident of birth. A bony old man was forced to crawl over a cobblestone street on his knees while soldiers beat him. My grandfather.

Large crowds of people were herded together, while Nazis walked among them collecting all wedding rings, gold teeth, or any precious metal. More precious than metal were the meanings and memories of those rings. Simply taken away. My parents' wedding rings could have been part of that desecration.

I'm sure there was more, but I was getting sick and turned it off. The lesson stayed. We think we are so permanently, automatically what

and who we are. Who would we be if the year were 1941 and the place Poland, the victims ourselves?

We think we could be no other way, for we have been no other way. In reality, we are but the summation of many variables over which we had no control. We are given.

What do you call a girl who is a school patrol boy? Whatever you call her, she was tending her corner in the lower downtown area. She was in, maybe, sixth grade. The wind blew crumpled paper and junk all around her. Her corner was also the corner of a porno movie house. I wonder what she thinks of the dirt and wind and, especially, the visible ulcer of man's sickness as she stands there.

"But why don't you want to grow up?"

This afternoon I said Mass at the detention home for the lost kids. Kids denied the simple ability to love. There was waged the whole battle of the cosmos in a microcosm. The whole relentless surge and thrust of creation and destruction in combat. I saw Christ *die* and rise.

Lord, you know Ralph, the 14-year-old lad. You heard him say he was going to get a jug of wine when released, so he could forget. At 14, he has *that* much to forget!

Here is a shadow without a substance, an echo without a call. Here is death before there was a living. But you *saw* his face when he held the chalice. You read his eyes when we spoke of God's love for him. He couldn't believe you would suffer so just for him. But the door began to open. The start of a dawn so great, so beautiful, the rebirth of a soul.

But also there in the class, mixed for the Mass, was a beautiful blond girl. Only you, Jesus, know the sorrow and misery of her story—of such a precious secret held in such little regard. Oh, Lord, she crushed me—her prayer was so *sincere!* She bowed her beautiful head and prayed so hard for "all the kids around the world who *need* your help, your love."

Either I'm blind, or for a space she was reaching, too—for a state of being where the inner person is of value. Two precious people—at a most sacred instant—both present to a dawning! But so clearly, Lord! So clearly! I saw the pain in Ralph; he was reaching for her. The urge, the fight, the struggle for giving respect he never knew, yet feels like the impression of a long lost dream. He wants more, Lord! But doesn't know what it is or how to have it. So true and real was the tension of the fight in him. What of her? A reform school uniform of tee shirt and jeans—so open. What does she feel? What subtle and everlasting effects are sinking into her of the meaning of man, love, life? How will she ever know the body is a harp, to be played by love's fingers?

And the Mass ended. They got up and left. Period.

Is it period, Jesus? Far from it. They go on. Every minute their lives go on. A note woven into the hymn. How will they fit? How does it balance to meaning? I saw you, Jesus, exist between those two, die and rise.

And this evening. Again I fed two of your lonely men on the road. Fed them and talked to them. Friends. Equals. Walking the same road. What strange and deep roads they have traveled and thus taken into themselves. Where do they fit? The harmony of the universe must sweep them up. But how?

◌◌◌◌◌◌

Mental wards are such haunted places. Patients glide around in their medicated fog vaguely talking about a reality they can't quite cope with. Slow motion. The elusive "answer" slips through their minds like a greased ball, always barely out of reach. You can silently hear each patient scream "I almost have it." Almost.

Last night Lynn didn't remember she had a husband or a three-month-old baby. Rhonda had attempted suicide by sticking her head in an oven. But first she took precautions that her demise would not ruin her curls. She didn't want to look ugly at her funeral. Eric was sporting not-too-old scar tissue on his wrists as well. But most

of the talk was about feeling useless, insecure, afraid—a sense of panic or having no place to go. All of the ordinary things that to them are extraordinary demons.

Coming home I heard Vikki Carr singing a beautiful love song on the radio. How violently the two realities collided. Or maybe they didn't collide; maybe they just vividly painted the two sides of the same reality. How many of you in Ward A would be there if all the elements of real love had surrounded you when you needed them? If the warmth of trust, the rain of tenderness, the cultivation of encouragement had attended your tree, would your branches not now be straight and tall?

In microcosm, the "one thing necessary" filled my mind, the common denominator to which every human variable can be reduced: to love and be loved. But there is more, a truth that is inexpressibly more! Someone must pay the price. To penetrate the eyes of those in Ward A is no small thing. Nor anyone else's, I think.

How easily, how blasphemously easy the word "love" comes to our lips.

Her face was so sad crowded into the tiny window of the door. So wrinkled and sad. The door was locked. The sign on it said "No Admittance." I wonder what the world looked like from her side?

The ward actually had two wings: one locked, one open. All day the face in the window watched the "guests" from the free ward walk around. They are at liberty to go to occupational therapy, the kitchen for coffee, or even, with doctor's permission, across the street to bowl or play bingo. Her side of the door is a different world. What goes on there? Or in the private universe of her mind? I wonder if her medication made slow-moving cartoons of us as we receded down the hall, or maybe blurred smudges of colored "stuff." Has that poor head received violent shocks of electricity in a search for certainty? What does she think? What haphazard combinations of tragic events brought her to her lonely post by the door of the world? Will she ever leave? And if she does, I wonder if she will find the free world any more free or sane than where

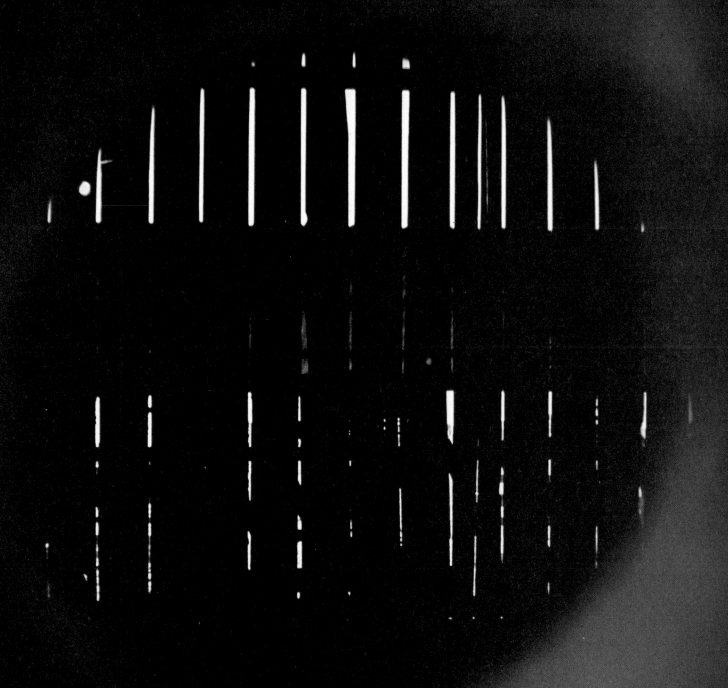

she is? Galaxies collide and fly apart on battle-fields so remote we can only imagine their existence, with such magnitude we cannot imagine, at times beyond our ability to reckon. Yet more powerful than these, for it is conscious, is the sadness of the little face by the door. And that face is more loved by her God than any star of the heavens. Does it matter at all, in any cosmic, universal economy, that I saw you there and so ardently hope for your peace. I hope so, because I do.

∽∽∽∽∽∽∽

Will he call the police tonight? Somewhere out in the dark Peter is struggling so hard to make that call. Poor little gnome. Nineteen and not five feet tall and a kleptomaniac.

Our conversation started the way so many others do, "I'm having trouble with the church. The changes and everything. I don't like it. In fact, at times I hate it!" Slowly it opened out where it usually does, "It's me I hate. Every day I get deeper and deeper in trouble. It's like digging my own grave and I can't stop." His particular demon was stealing. Anything. Whether he needed it or not. Within the last year it has been money. Money because people seemed to care more about money than anything else. How do you stop before you commit a felony and end up in jail or in a rehabilitation center? How on earth do you stop so you don't have to look at a world made ugly by seeing it through a haze of self-hatred.

As he came, he left. Opened the car door and disappeared into the night. A tiny, pudgy figure disappearing around the corner. He had decided to seek professional help. Is he sick and tired enough of being sick and tired to really reach out? Can he?

He is out there now, somewhere, fighting the biggest battle of his life. Bring him home, Lord. Bring him from Friday to Easter Sunday.

∽∽∽∽∽∽∽

Eva girl, I really hope you make it. I wish all the confidence, protection and good will you have gained from your stay in the psych ward would form around you like a protective bubble. It will, for awhile. Then it will fade as energy fades from a long-distance runner, leaving you defenseless; and that isn't good, especially when you have the terrible handicap of so much tough-looking beauty.

Beauty has many faces. The experiences we live through have much to say of the particular brand any one individual may have. I don't know your book, Eva, but I do know you have for now won your battle with drugs. You aren't so sure about alcohol. It has led you into many meat grinders, but you aren't quite as ready to see it as you are other drugs. No rings are on your fingers, but you know all about the body-on-body bit. You are still a teen-ager, but aren't going home, so that must be a bad scene. Your head is all screwed back on; your eyes are clear and your smile radiant. But there is something else left in you by all the painful, growing experience you have had that is as apparent as a shooting star at night.

I don't know what to call it, but I hope it doesn't destroy you. You are going to find a lot of pushers you don't know are going to ask you if you want a hit. Just because you look like you might. Dozens of beautiful women could walk down the street and some moral midget with his brains in other places than his head will insult only you with his verbalized stupidity. Why you? Out of all these women, why you? Because you look hard and wild. The footprints of where you have been are reflected in your face and walk. Frustration will cramp your heart so often as imbeciles try to drag you down. They won't care where you want, and are trying, to go. They will only see what to them looks like an easy mark, a chick who is looking for it. And with frustration comes doubt. When you are insulted so often you will begin to wonder, "Maybe I am what they say." With doubt the door swings slowly open. All the way back to the ward.

Beautiful, lovely Eva, you are so happy now under your protective bubble. Getting out. Your smile so genuine. If only you can find some help.

Streets, a most precious, vulnerable, tough-looking girl will soon be back. You can easily destroy her. But why? What does it prove but that you are more insane than the patients of a mental ward. Please be kind.

∽∾∽∾∽∾∽

Poor Heidi, she tried so hard not to cry but she didn't make it. The more she talked about her eighth grade classmate and friend, the more filmy her eyes became. Pretty soon fullblown, gigantic tears splashed on her blue poncho. But then, any person hooked on drugs who is also a pusher, especially one in eighth grade, is worth crying about. Heidi wants it all to go away, make it so it doesn't exist. If only it could.

One of her grade school customers took too much or got some bad stuff and went deaf. Weird though it is, drug addiction can go unnoticed, but not sudden deafness. Forced into action and awareness the sewer backed up all the way to the evil pusher. The ". . . little, evil eighth grade pusher." Now what? What of the deaf girl and all the other clients? Do you mind if I cry with you, Heidi? And I am as helpless as you.

∽∾∽∾∽∾∽

June's thirteen-year-old daughter ran away last week. "The days aren't too bad," she said, "you can keep your mind full of other things. Besides, for some reason you don't think of terrible things happening during the day. It's the nights that kill you. All I can think about is where Becky is and what may be happening to her."

Even if it doesn't destroy Becky, it will June.

∽∾∽∾∽∾∽

Thursday night Tom and I put the hood over our stove. Friday night he went to a movie with his wife, Pat. Saturday night the demon won—

he blew his brains out all over the kitchen floor.

Tom, some relative of yours was there cursing you, "Stupid! Stupid!" was all he could say. Your neighbor condemned you for putting Pat and your kids through this ordeal. All Pat could do was blame herself. Your parents will blame her. In their pain they must blame someone.

Everyone was so miserable. But, I am thinking, none so miserable as you when you staggered home drunk. None so helplessly sick as you, or depressed when you looked in Pat's eyes and knew that you had failed again.

My God, what horrible black wastes you have stumbled through these past years. Oh, yes, you fought. Especially this last month. You helped us start our brand new AA Group. You took your family places, tried to meet each day with joy. But the demon was never far behind, was he, Tom? How many times did you stop the flow of energy required to struggle for your sobriety, and hopelessly state, "I can't." Did you always know you wouldn't make it? Did you never think the spiritual awakening just might happen? Maybe not, yet how gamely you tried. I've seen many try but it seemed to me no man ever fought harder or suffered more.

And now it is between you and your merciful God. What a relief to know he understands.

Even in what seems so tragic, there is still good to be found. As you lay on your kitchen floor, Tom, covered with the police blanket, a young 19-year-old stood by me looking down. The same demon inhabits his soul. He is wise enough to know it is no joke, but maybe doesn't realize how deadly serious it is. Your blood said much to him. If nothing else, maybe that boy will not have to lie headless on some floor in years to come. Maybe at least that. How restless you were. How tormented.

Tom, rest in peace.

Saturday—The Day of Fire

"KINDLE IN THEM THE FIRE
OF YOUR LOVE AND THEY SHALL
RECREATE THE EARTH"

Dark. It is so
dark—said the
man. No, said
his friend. It is
only the time before
light catches the
world again.

Daybreak, like a waterfall of liquid light, cascades over the heights of life. Not once. Not for an hour. But for a moment that is now and never becomes past. The presence of the New Fire is melting snow high in the mountains that feeds the living falls bit by bit. Yet never a drop is lost; each is important.

The quivering moment of anticipation has not been more than the treasure it promised. For to stand in the light of the waterfall is greater than the power to dream of it.

Lord Jesus, Come in Glory, shouted the early Brothers.

~~~~~~~~~

Blessed are the pure of heart—the innocent. And we look to those who have never done anything. Who have resisted like brave iron soldiers. Today I looked into the eyes of a girl from the projects. They were filled with tears that ran down her cheeks. But what hadn't these eyes seen, who hadn't owned her face. The eyes were so tired for she had been up all night. No home, parole officer after her, no clothes but what were on her back, no money. No nothing, but a sickness of life. So truly pure, as Tennessee Williams' people are pure. Pure because she hungers so for love. If it were ever presented to her, she would take it and never let it go. This is purity, for it is the unborn God in us, striving for birth. Slut, whore, how many names has she been called. But God has chosen the weak to confound the strong. And He said the thieves and prostitutes will enter heaven before the "chosen" for "blessed are the pure of heart, for they shall see God." Yes, you shall.

God protect her.

~~~~~~~~~

"God, your sea is so great—my boat is so small." At times the waves are so high and the pitiful little boat of my life pitches and rolls. I do not wish it to sink. No sooner does one storm abate and my boat momentarily eases into placid waters, then again the winds blow turning the sky black. Again the thunder of ignorance and pride booms like a frightening drum while the lightning of passion and irresponsibility would eliminate what little progress seems to have been made. Yet no matter what, God, I do not wish it to sink. Nor, I think, does anyone.

~~~~~~~~~

Johnny taught me a great thing tonight: appreciation. This was one of the first warm days so I asked him if he wanted to go visit friends. He went bananas—so I put his wheel chair in the car and off we went. Big deal—visit some friends. But that is the point. It is! If routine has not dulled the reality.

After an hour or so, we went for a walk around the block. Everything was a huge wonder. When something caught his eye he would plant his feet, like anchors, and point his one good hand at whatever amazed him. Once it was a pet pigeon walking on a family's window sill. One of the kids held the bird while Johnny stroked it, wildly excited. A plane flying high overhead evoked sounds of pure delight. So did a motorcycle that roared by and some boys shooting baskets by a garage. But the most thrilling adventure of all were the three girls who stopped and talked. It was the people who really thrilled Johnny. New faces, new voices, new eyes to look into. And don't think he doesn't see!

Before we left, John had a root beer float. A little pop and ice cream. But no, it was more than that. Someone cared enough to fix it for him; Dorothy Mae held the straw. That is rare. Someone who cares. John misses little of what's around him. He appreciates all he sees. How blind are those who see too freely.

~~~~~~~~~

It is a nothing day. It is as common and ordinary as dirt. No big holiday, no special month. Yet any day can be special—a day of New Fire. This day can find the heavy layers of night roll back while the red and gold tide of flame advances on your kingdom. Fear can be put to flight. Insecurity can dissolve into self-confidence, ignorance into wisdom. Prison doors sealed a hundred years can fly open deep within the for-

gotten ground of your soul, liberating the rightful heirs to your throne. While the counterfeit demons who seized power can be put to death.

As the New Fire, lava-like, flows over your planet, the icy cold is penetrated. There is a warmth that bubbles up from within, radiating from hand and eye. Whatever the source of the tingling heat, it transforms everything you encounter. What has been deadly routine takes on meaning; countless magnificent spectacles never seen before now greet you as you pass; the masks of people you considered selfish or stupid melt before the New Fire, leaving only the real face of those you encounter. At once you see they are not evil or malicious—they are just people as yet untouched by the fire trying to do the best they can.

New Fire is not only a gift of God. It is God. God as he imparts his power to create and re-create life within one another. New Fire is the reality of love, the truth of the Eucharist, the meaning of life over death. It is man's only acceptable gift back to his God. He who would give such a gift, he who would break this bread, will

carry mankind's greatest dreams and sorrows within him. To give the lightning of New Fire to another is to live within that person forever.

It can happen. It does happen. Perhaps today.

God, being Spirit, has no face. But the Spirit who is God is capable of being seen and touched by emanating through the material world. Which is the only way spirit can ever be encountered by mortal man. How many times this day I saw and loved God's beautiful face.

Lauri's long black hair hangs almost to her waist. Even at 12, confidence pours from her like water from Niagara. So deep and alive shine her brown eyes. At our picnic she came over, pointed to a huge slide and flatly declared, "You are chicken to go down that slide, I bet. Besides, your bottom is probably too big." Then she just turned and walked toward the towering toy. She won, of course. We had a race there; she won a second time. Such a lovely invitation she offered me, a privilege to go down the slide with her. God's face is very young and innocent.

Tom also has long hair. Not as long as Lauri's and it is blond. Tom's brilliant tie-dyed shirt of purple, yellow and white is a perfect reflection of his spirit—deep and bright. But not his body. Tom lives in a wheel chair. What strikes me most about Tom is not his crystal clear eyes or sensitive face—more than these, the gentleness of his voice. It is very calm, very soft. I don't know the circumstances that brought him to his chair, but I do know he feels it super-sensitively. His conversation is about poetry, politics and world affairs. God's face is immensely gentle and serene. In Tom it also has but 23 years.

Lu has about 55 years. Long hair and tie-dyed clothes are as far from her as duplicity is from Lauri or cruelty from Tom. But how she can love. Happiness and excited joy bubbled from her pudgy face because Kathy went upstairs with the Al Ateen kids. Lu has taken responsibility for this group of kids from alcoholic homes. Responsibility to her means they all live inside her. Kathy had been hanging around for over a month. She was far more sullen and bitter than fourteen years should make anyone. Even a daughter of a vagrant alcoholic father and an unbalanced mother who never stopped running. Lu's group was putting on a skit for their local AA Club. Suddenly, ten minutes before it started, Kathy darted up the stairs and into the room where they were practicing. One tiny, slip of a girl with a "carry it on" patch sewn to her back pocket. Lu had no words or way to express her joy and relief. But it showed in her face. God's face—which is overflowing with a mother's love.

Duram looks like a derelict Santa Claus. Huge glowing silver-grey beard. Old bib overalls cover his legs, one of which was amputated somewhere below the knee. He wears a cheap grey suit coat, as well. Duram quietly sits in the rehabilitation center with the rest of the "guests" in the chemical dependency program. A talk is in progress. It is about self-honesty being the only door leading to sanity. He kind of listens. No one really knows but him. Most of the time he looks at the floor. I catch his eye for a second. Only that. The glance of a lonely, tormented man who sees no chance for tomorrow. Is it raining in your soul, Duram? God's face is lined and stamped with such utter agony.

The sky is blood red, the sea is boiling, winds of pure energy are opening the tombs of every man's head and heart—the face of God is everywhere.

Real people have joy.

The head of Carver Settlement House has been there thirty years. I don't imagine anyone in the world is more taken up with the hurtfulness of this world than he. From the other side of God's face he lives there, works there, most of all he loves there.

Such a hopeless situation. But he has joy. He radiates happiness. And so does Tom who runs the local halfway house. *Genuine*. Not in a sense that has never been tried. But joy bearing the scars of ten million wounds, joy that is stronger than pain, joy that knows the rhythm of a futureless present and still rejoices.

What, then, is their joy? Of what is it made?

Certainly of the proposition that some force greater than man rules the whole scene. That this life and what it carries is only part of the whole. Certainly to the proposition that the highest a man can strive for is effort—not results. For what more can you give but your life to the effort. And after you are spent and even your shadow is gone, the shacks and high-rises and people who can't and don't understand, will still remain. Those people seemingly born to lose will be here a hundred years after their shadow is

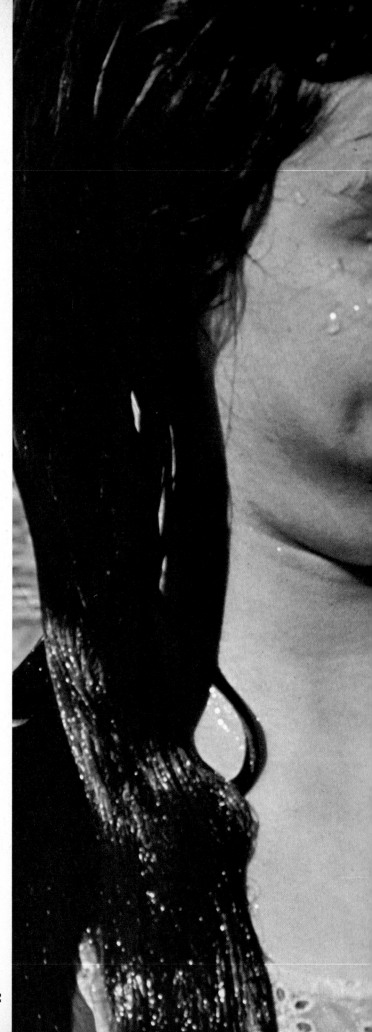

gone. But the effort, the effort has been made.

But what a vast chasm between knowing this and believing it. The knowledge must first get its blood bath; and the resurrection, if there is one, is calm joy.

Joy is the pain, the belief that a greater force will take your effort, like an arrow, and shoot it through the world to some yet-to-come land, carrying many people on its shaft. Joy is an arrow.

But then again, maybe it is something else. Something different.

One evening while sitting in the cramped, poorly-furnished attic apartment of a Mennonite church talking to a young married couple doing "in service" work for the church, I discovered a new definition. Art, the young man with the thin beard and quick, joyful tongue, put it this way, "Joy, to me, is the constant, pain-filled cry of every living human being. A plea to be heard, to be noticed and loved. Joy is the rare moment when, during the pain, the cry breaks through and someone momentarily hears it. Joy is being heard, and on a deeper level, being the one who hears. It is felt, and the closeness of humanity is painful, hopeful and filled with wonder."

Downstairs in the tiny, tattered church, another member of the "in service" group was teaching the local youth group songs. Easter songs.

I think Art has created a lot of joy—and found even more.

Civilization, like sanity, is a most tenuous quality.

In a conversation last night, a man mused why the Indian has made such little progress in the area of civil rights, while the black has done comparatively well. He was answered with "because the Indian is no threat. If he had tried to burn down Detroit and Los Angeles, he would be getting what the blacks are."

Aside from all ethical considerations about violence or patriotic rhetoric about "all men are created equal," the answer is probably correct. History shows little or no evidence that *any* society is going to give its minority groups rights or a share in power unless they take it. Unless

threatened, there is no real concern. Is civilization the same as cultural maturity? If so, this would indicate we are about five years old. It also outlines in the most stark contrast exactly what New Fire is and its supreme need within the heart of a culture. You cannot be more than you are simply of yourself. If your light is too weak to expel the darkness and no New Fire comes from without, then you are condemned to darkness.

"And the light shines in the darkness. . . ."

Dale had been counting on going to the zoo for weeks. So I guess I was only surprised by the depth and wonder of the kiss he gave me, rather than the fact that he did. It came at such a funny time, too, just as I was about to throw him in the seal tank. In the confusion of getting off the bus, he wound up in the wrong wheel chair. This buggy had no foot rests so his legs kept getting stubbed on the ground as we rolled along. Trouble Smith turned out to be the rustler. We caught up to her at the seal tank. Her legs are bent in such a way they never touch the ground. Trouble's gleaming, dancing eyes told loud and clear how funny she thought her little heist was. In picking Dale up to return each to his own, I was about to toss him to the seals when he planted a wet, wonderful one on me. How are you going to throw a guy to the fish after that!

Dale's face portrays the total spectrum of innocent human sweetness to suffering. Sometimes when you look at him, all you can see are his huge, luminous eyes. The delicacy of his face, combined with the immense vulnerability of his hypnotic eyes, makes for a perfect portrayal of a weeping angel.

But then, what is an angel? Is Joe an angel?

I read an article from *Harpers* on life inside San Quentin. The stabbings and murder are so common it makes no difference at all except that you might be next. It spoke of the tensions and unbelievably "different" world it is. A world so degrading, so brutal, it destroys all whom it touches.

Joe wrote today. He spent five years in a state penitentiary. "A knife? Hell, yes, I had one. A

little three-incher I wore on my neck. No one was going to mess up my face." Joe knows all about it. He is a miracle. Straight as a string, working, supporting a family, totally out of trouble. Fifteen were on parole with him. He alone didn't go back. There was even a little plastic "Smile" button in his letter. Talk about a token from a different world.

Some say luck. Some call it God. Some say it's just a matter of time. How about it, Joe, what do you say? Are you a work of art formed in the forge of New Fire? And if so, what of your middle-aged sister hitchhiking back home to her poor house?

She was a heavy black woman returning from charwork in a wealthy suburb. Her name was Sula. She looked like some type of a huge out-of-place Christmas ornament. Her coat was shabby red and her hat, perched on her kinky head, was a torn, faded green.

As it turned out, she only lived three blocks from the rectory. After she got over the shock of a Catholic priest picking her up, she began to tell me about her conversion. In her purse was the handy little black Bible she knew almost by heart. When she spoke about her conversion, there was nothing else in the world. Her spirit filled the car.

"It's jus' like the Lord comin' down and takin' hold a ya, Father. I used to be a sinful woman, but then the Lord came and I jus' couldn't say nothin' to Him but 'yes.' And I been converted ever since."

The closer we got to Easton and her home, the more excited she became talking about Jesus, her conversion, and reading the Good Book. When it came time to let her off, I'll never forget her parting, excited statement, "Altarman, honey baby, I'm gonna pray for you. Yes, I sure am. And I am gonna get my whole congregation to pray for you because you're a good man." I can't think of anyone I would rather have praying for me.

Dale, Joe, Sula, all so different, yet bearing the same mark of the Craftsman and his fearsome fire.

M104 is part of a spiral nebulae within a galaxy 40 million light-years away. I am looking at a picture of it. It is called "the sombrero" due to its shape. A flat golden dish with burning white hub existing in cold black space 40 million light-years away. Perhaps it no longer exists. The very light needed to expose the film for this picture has been searching this tiny camera on this speck of dust called Earth for 40 million light-years. Before any intelligent living thing existed on Earth, it started its journey. The sombrero itself is but part of a galaxy consisting of millions of suns as does our own. Each sun gathering around itself its own solar system. Beyond that galaxy are another 40 million light-years, another billion stars, and another 40 million beyond that. And another beyond that.

What matter in all that time and space one face in a mental ward door, one ride in a crippled boy's chair, one deed done with honor, though the price was high. It verges on gross insanity to remotely think that one act done on mediocre Earth could possibly count for less than anything. Or one life for that matter. Or all the combined lives of every animate being who ever did or will live in Planet Earth's history. A history so shortly begun and soon to end by galactic time. Time which loses all meaning for human minds on so grand a timepiece. But it does matter.

The face *does* count. And so the honorable deed. And every second of our lives that thunders from one galaxy to the next. For the Creator of every ounce of matter, every throb of energy, walked our hills and sat by our rivers. The universe dwelt within him, obediently fulfilling its course. But without conscious love. Love is the heartbeat of the galaxies, that alone which gives it conscious meaning and purpose. A nebula cannot love. Man—fallible, finite, utterly limited man, has been endowed by the Creator to be the tongue by which the hymn of the universe may be sung.

How grand our role.

ᘓ∕ᘐ∕ᘓ∕ᘐ∕ᘓ∕ᘐ∕ᘓ

"Shalom." "Peace of the Lord be with you." What is peace? After the death, Christ came to

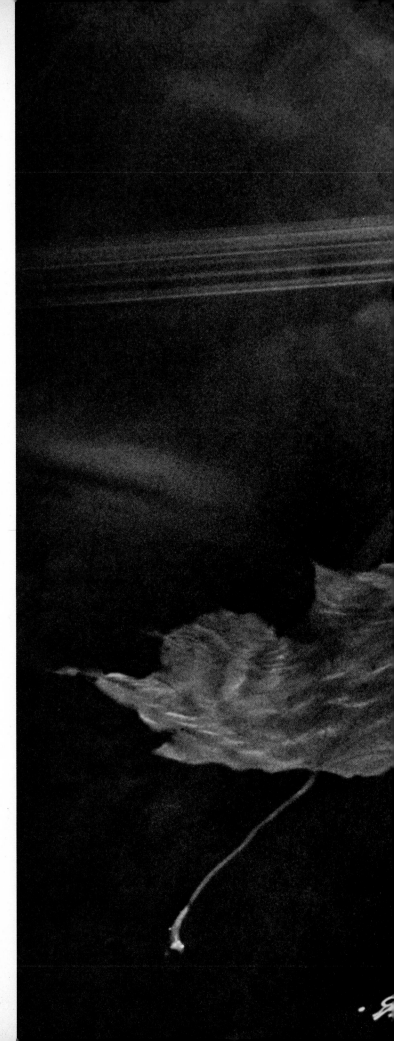

the chosen ones several times and always said, "Peace be to you." Always. "He stood in the midst of them." He stood before all they were, all they saw, all they thought and would do, and said, "Peace."

Lord, I see not you before me but a chalice, a chalice open to every movement of our existence. And from this vast throng, from this ever-changing orb of energy, I see, drop by drop, the chalice coming to fullness. Is this not what you gave your chosen? Is this not "peace"? Certainly not ease, not mere joy, it is anything but a stopping of labor. Peace is the experience of not being satisfied while retaining the intense desire to strive. It is the sight of the sap of life dropping, pearl by pearl, into the chalice.

Yet peace is not a huge blanket, is it Lord? It is a thread, an unending thread constantly being woven into the wedding garment we shall wear to the feast. Peace is having your heart broken by being loved too much; it is hearing the echo of love shimmer from another mountain; it is seeing a reflection in another's stream in your heart and visiting the sunset-coolness in another's valley. Peace is seeing a flower across a wide and torturous chasm and starting out for it, even though you see the blood, your blood, on the rocks below before you are asked to spill it. Peace is an ache, a hunger, deeper than joy or pain; it is the beat in the heart of love. And the ache is because others cannot share, the hunger to have them share. An unbroken thread.

When Our Lord bequeathed the chosen peace, he "breathed on them," imparted life to them. In their hearts they became conscious of the chalice, of the dripping of their own vision. This is peace. They preached, they were rejected, ad-mired, reverenced, hated and hounded; they were stoned and flogged—with whips and with love as well; they bled because others would not love and because they loved too much; they were destroyed on crosses, flayed alive, thrown into pots of oil and from their own temples. And through it all ran a thread woven into their hearts, "Peace be to you." Peace through it all— for *always* there was the chalice, always the dripping, whether it be the red of love, the white of joy, the violet of penance, the dark chaos of hate. And when, like James, they hurtled off the temple roof, what supreme joy—for they fell in totality, with all their life, back to the chalice from which they gathered existence. They became the pearl dropping. The mystery of peace. Where charity and love prevail, there is God.

New Fire gives no new words to the song of life. Rather, it gives new meaning to old words rendering what before was common and routine, exquisite, new. New Fire peels back the protective coating of the everyday, revealing a resplendent inner core.

New Fire has a million forms, comes in endless names, singing every song man can conceivably hear. New dawn is limited only by the kinds of darkness through which men live. Just before the dawn the earth is quiet. All that can be heard is the pulsing heartbeat of every living thing. The trees, flowers and water reverently hush their search. It is quiet, calm. Waiting for the fire to touch the horizon.

Sunday—Day of All Living

"WHO WILL ROLL AWAY THE STONE"

I fell in love with a most beautiful girl today. I held her in my arms and knew this was a treasure like none other in the universe. Her name is Cecelia, or CeCe. Her hair is long and blond. Her blue jeans and brown boots were just what a 16-year-old girl should wear. But her serenity and courage far exceed what anyone can expect of a teen-ager.

Some fifteen months ago her neck was broken in a swimming accident. CeCe is quite paralyzed from the neck down. Together we were invited to give several talks at a local high school. Wheeling her down the crowded, fad-crammed corridors, there was no hint of bitterness or sorrow about her. Some of the kids were short, some tall. Some right-handed, some left-handed. She was handicapped. That's all. I felt so proud being with her.

CeCe doesn't play around. She made a few opening remarks about the center where she lives. Then flat out asked how they felt about handicapped people. When someone said they felt sorry for them, she asked why. Which seemed like a dumb question. Not to CeCe. She quietly and quickly explained the facts of life. "It's a matter of being tough," she said. "If you are tough you make it. If not, you die."

"Making it" means still loving life, caring, building enthusiasm, hoping for tomorrow. Not "making it" is drowning in self-pity, keeping stoned all the time, harboring resentment and fear. The weak die. So simple.

As for CeCe, "I love life," she said. When I picked her limp body out of the chair to put her in the car, I wanted to just hold her forever. How precious can one person be. Yet I am *so* helpless. Not just to change anything, but to adequately, in any way, tell her or everyone else of what a magnificent meaning "human" can have.

∞∞∞∞∞

I see the world spread out in a two-fold garden. Each half clearly marked; each clearly identifiable as being one or the other of the only two flowers growing in the garden of all living. Each was either basically a giver or a taker. Strength born of wisdom won through struggle was the difference. Those who had acquired such precious wisdom understood it was fluid. Either it grew or diminished daily. It never remained the same. The condition of its growth was the willingness to share what had been won. Refusal to allow others to drink from the well immediately rendered it dry as dust. Whereas, it grew deeper and sweeter in direct proportion to the

number who freely found access. Therefore, the givers seemed always in a controlled rush to give of their treasure.

Some of the most unlikely flowers wore the mark of the giver upon their heads. They were sealed with the blood of the lamb. In contrast to these were the ones who by profession or role should have worn the blood of the lamb, but did not. There was no urgency about them, none of the confidence or deep-seated light that glows up from the furnace of wisdom. There was just an outer appearance and a job. But without the seal of wisdom, the external appearance deceived no one.

Barb, many would say, is just the wife of a foolish drunk. She has no official title, no economic or political power, no office to uphold. In the annals of the greats of the world you would not find her name even in a footnote. Maybe not. But there she sat in her high white boots, blue and white dotted dress, pulling Margie inch-by-inch out of the swamp of hopeless despair she had allowed her alcoholic husband to put her in. Barb belonged to Al Anon, that beautiful group of givers who render to each other sanity and a chance to live even if their spouses choose to die. Barb's whole person is a hugely electric magnet affecting anyone who comes close enough. Margie isn't going to die.

All kinds of people milled around drinking coffee and chatting small talk. But not at that table. Over there life and death were wrestling. Presently, Gert walked over and sat down. Now the score was 2 to 1 in favor of givers. Gert had come in before Mass and said, "Peace of Christ be with you." She meant it. She also knew Christ was the prime giver and "peace" is of the nature of all giving, growing in proportion as you give it away. Gert was there to give. She started pitching right in.

The only thing better than 2 is 3. Joy came over next. Now it was 3 to 1. You don't get those odds often. She brought her own brand of suffering and wisdom. Add that to Barb and Gert and among the chitchat there was more solid life going Margie's way than she had ever known.

Kathy saw this gathering of the clan and walked over with her cup of coffee and ocean of greatness. Few have ever walked the roads she has or come back from so far in the shadows. Shortly before, she, as all the rest, was not a giver nor could have been. Before joining the pool of strength and wisdom that Al Anon is, they were going in so many directions they had nothing to give. But Kathy got it together and now every bad thing that happened is a source of power for others. All that misery is a slingshot that now catapults light to the extent—the immense extent—to which the shadows existed. Sheila left her group and came over to join her sisters. Add her sunshine and the energy boomed. Al Anon and helping Margie bloom into a giver is what they all lived for. The core of their energy. It is God, Christ, holiness and grace in operation.

And there was Margie, a life raft with no air, sitting among a super-energized group of living sacraments. No one else knew or saw the miracle going on at that table. The transformation from fragmentation to spiritual unity had begun again. Lightning jumping from one pole to another. Easter happening.

Maybe in a short lapse of time another observer looking over the field of the living will notice a change has been made. One that was a gaping wound had been made whole, one who was a lost pilgrim has found serenity called Home. And that pilgrim's name will be Margie. Perhaps this future observer will write in his mind or on paper, "Margie stretched out a saving road to another who was lost and motioned her to follow, for she knows it is the way Home." Maybe he will thrill to see the miracle of human growth start again. Margie giving life as it was given to her.

Moe—I ask you—where shall a man take his stand? I guess every man must answer that for himself. But you, my brother, have raised your flag with those who have no one else. Others with reasonable, justified cause will march with those who have much company, who not only are in the spotlight but own it. You march to a different tune.

I see in my mind's eye legions of individuals who are unwanted. Those who are not even a cause for others to practice piety on. I have seen them dwelling in your love many times. Their

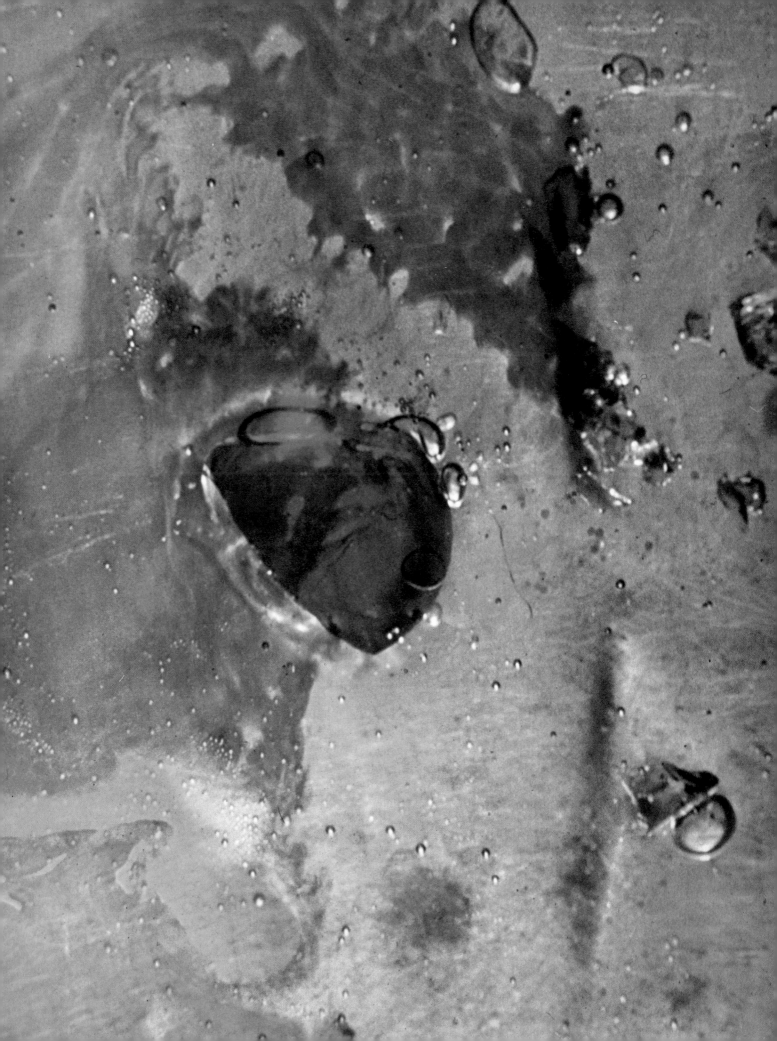

compelling beauty has spoken to you in words few others hear. Your response to their life has drawn you into so many "strange" situations. Yet you always return. And always will till one day you die in the street where you have loved.

⟪∿∿∿∿∿∿⟫

Officer Perry is quite a man. His new orthopedic shoe shines like a cat's eye and the steel on his brace is equally as bright. Without this hook-up he can't elevate his foot. Most of the muscles in his right leg are severely injured. It was a gift from a car thief who smashed up the vehicle after stealing it. Just as Perry's squad car arrived, the boy threw it in reverse and rammed the police car. Perry had his leg out the door.

The last thing Perry says he remembers as they took him away in the ambulance was a crowd of kids cheering and chanting, "Kill all pigs."

Perry said he'd sure like to meet the kid who gave him this permanent gift. He's back out on the streets now. He got thirty days in a home of correction. "It's like a townhouse," says Perry. "I know lots of kids who like to go there because it's so much better than their homes."

Then he paused, "Hell, I hope the kid had a good time there. No doubt it was a lot better than he's used to." Then he got talking about Star . . .

He was answering a call one night when this beautiful chick comes running up to him, arms wide open. She was shaking so he put her in the back of the squad car and turned the heat on. Her chill was inside. Star was ten feet high on drugs. Her boyfriend ambled up. He had given her the stuff, but didn't know how much. He didn't know, or care. What did he look like, a doctor for Christ's sake? Star was on the downward slide of her high by the time Perry got her to a hospital. When he carried her in, everything inside her came out all over him. Perry stuck with her, though. All the way to the ward he was by her side. He said he almost cried when she started playing in her drippings on the floor with her foot. She was laughing. Several days later when he visited Star and told her how she looked and what she did, her only remark was, "It is beautiful. Isn't it beautiful!" Today she is the biggest pusher in her part of town. Physically, she is withered.

Perry's bum leg is going to keep him out of a squad car—maybe forever. And that is a tragic loss. Really.

⟪∿∿∿∿∿∿⟫

How many times a person can be born! The

little girl at the reform school after confession said, "I've been reborn." Do you hear, World, you who look down on black skin, on delinquents, on the wild ones? Do you hear her words? "Reborn." You may not be able to read, girl; you will never hear the words of the great theologians of the church, but you understand them. Far deeper than many a priest or "good" person. You understand birth and sin—sacrament. You know your Lord. Girl, I share your joy. You have filled my cup. You have banished so much of my pain. The river will continue to flow—the waters both bitter and sweet, but the sun sets today on a world where one child of God has said in the joy of her Lord—I have been reborn.

Would that we could all know as much as you.

∽∾∽∾∽∾∽

This evening I truly felt and saw God's skin. The mystery of the skin of your loved one. The skin festered and broken in a thousand wounds, the skin smeared and sticky in countless unwashed parts, the skin hard and cracked bearing the scars of wounds deeper than blood. But tonight I touched and thrilled to the enfolding beauty of God's skin in black. The black of a smooth brow over which flowed the waters of Baptism—the moment of pure openness to the pulse of grace. The black of poverty-stricken skin which bore the marks of the Sacrament, black eyes that see the corrupt man-degraded world of the slums, but now incorporated into the Body of Christ, the black of ears that hear the noise and disharmony of poverty, the nose that smells filth, the black skin stretched over a heart that beats in God's lost outpost. And black is beautiful. Black is the newest extension of Christ in this world; black is the just-born pouring his touches and visions and smells into the life-flow of his new family. Black is Earl; black is the Body of Christ; black is the skin I touched this night; and richer, much richer, is the family because of it.

Too much do you give, Lord.

∽∾∽∾∽∾∽

Who is wise? Who experiences? Liturgy—communication—sign—human. Words. Who knows their meaning? Who is wise?

The pit is a mud hole actually groaning with huge, animal-like machines. Drilling, pounding, pushing a building up from nothing. Jocko worked in the pit. Just an ordinary construction worker, sloshing around in the mud.

In the morning he stands before the hole, stretches and summons up the work his hands must do. The labor of his back and arms, his whole body. Just to prove that he is. "I am God," he says, as he lifts the planks and feels the dawn warm to noon. "I am God because I am making where nothing was before. And when this poor old body is dust in the grave, this here building that's made of my bone and sweat will be here. Because of this building, I can't die. Man, I own time."

Across the street many learned people read big books. They tell each other how man must become man so he can know God.

At night Jocko sat in his broken chair rocking his son in his lap. The breeze on his bare chest was a language he deeply understood. The language of belonging to all that is. The words of seeing what is and letting it know you. It spoke of rest now that he had paid his debt of strain to the day. The night touched him. In his son, his eyes saw back to the past. In his grasp was the momentary stop of the on-rush of history. All his history from the time they hunted with spears till they settled in the tribes of modern cities. He spoke no words, thought no individual thoughts. There was only the hugely deep reality of a man and his son.

Later, in harmony with all the mystery and magic of the night, he gave himself with a great burst of joy and searching to the woman he loved. In the sharing they created each other.

At the university, a heated debate broke out in the elegant lounge on the meaning of Sacrament. The truth of grace and God's revelation. Then the professional students retired to their rooms, read for a time and went to sleep.

Next morning, back in the womb of the huge building, Jocko looked up at the students watching the construction. He vaguely saw their books he couldn't read. He saw their badges of status, their collars and quick manners, which said in

sharp terms, "I am. Obviously. Don't you see that? Please, see that I am!" Jocko could almost smell their money and breeding. He knew they would use this building like a shell after he had given it birth.

"Look how smart those people be," he thought, "what do you suppose they study in those big books. Must be powerful stuff."

Then he turned back to his labor, back to lifting and moving and building. Yet he felt so deeply cut off from a world he figured he would never understand—have no part in. The world of deep speculation.

Who is wise?

On this lovely night let me share with you a dream. There will be a going home, a time when pieces fit.

On that day blind little Jill who had to get two inches from the mailbox to see it, will walk in the sunshine. The street down by Pruitt Igoe where we tried to move Tan and her mom, who already had gone, will shine as diamonds. Winky will be ten feet tall and Stanley will win the Olympics. On that day all the night people we know so well will not be afraid of the sun and CeCe will dance till dawn. Since our paths parted we have met so many others. I don't know the treasures you've met along your way, but I know they are yours. And being yours, are mine. At times my heart aches for you to share the beauty the Lord has sent me. You would understand so well. You know there are so many worlds all around us. You have more than one yardstick. You have never met Don, Randy, Cecelia or Tommy. But you would love them. They march alone.

On that day we will all be together. Every little person on Earth. The others can do what they want, but we will be together.

I saw the widow drop her mite into the box tonight. Hundreds of people streamed in. The widow in this case was recently separated from her husband. Friends were hard to come by. Hesitantly she looked around and quietly slipped three nickels into the basket. I guess the basket being out was a surprise because no one put any envelopes in it. A huge round basket holding only three nickels. Somehow it seemed awfully full.

Ideas are like diamonds littering our streets, homes and cities. Every so often someone who has more or less risen above routine blindness stumbles over one and "discovers" it. His wild shouts of enthusiasm soon bring others who share in the new-found wealth. Everyone feels immensely wealthy and quite proud. And so gloriously strut down the diamond-lined road, celebrating the light, even while passing up the vast majority of wisdom scattered all around him.

A huge black-bearded patient named Tiny at the chemical dependency center told me today that every living man is both handicapped and rich. Handicapped, because everyone has his own prison—rich, because everyone has his own key. Freedom, he says, is finding it.

Lord, I would go diamond hunting in the dark today.

Discussion Guide

The following suggestions for group discussions and projects have been planned to bring about fuller participation, and through this a better understanding of the major points made in this book.

Each participant should have a personal copy of the book for use during sessions and at home between sessions. Each participant should be encouraged to read the book through in its entirety, make marginal notes as he or she progresses and then review these notes upon completion of the book.

Seven sessions are suggested (or number of sessions could be lessened or increased depending on the progress of the group, their in-depth interest and time limitations). A preliminary meeting should be planned for distribution of the book followed by a broad outline by the leader as to how the group will progress. Reading assignment of one section to be read and re-read should be made in preparation for the second meeting especially related to the questions for Section 1. The more pre-group effort made by each individual, the more spontaneous will be the discussion at each session.

WEEK OF FIRE is both a visual and a verbal experience—and as such stress should be laid on both the words of the author and the "visual theology" of the photography. In general, meditation should be invited on the pictures as they relate to the subject matter and to the individual (and group) position in life.

Groups should be relatively small. If for example there is a large discussion group or class, these should be divided into smaller groups of no more than fifteen people each. Each group would discuss among themselves the chapter under discussion and then would be brought together for group leader comment, questions or observations. Create and maintain a relaxed atmosphere in each session. Encourage group confidence and tolerance so each person accepts the other where the other is at the moment and not where he or she should be.

With seven sessions, the opening meeting should be one of introduction, mood creation and general instructions on the program planned. The following seven sessions would take up one section at a time (key questions follow for these chapter sessions for the leader's use to bring out the important points in each chapter). The final session should be a recapitulation of the outstanding ideas that have been expressed by the group.

Agenda

First Session:

Read "Emmaus Bound" Section (Pages 4-11)

1. How do you see your role as a pilgrim Christian?
2. In what way can we say that religious terms such as Crucifixion, Resurrection, Eucharist, Easter are also descriptions of our human experiences?
3. Discuss your own experiences of Christ dying and rising in the world around you.
4. Why do you feel it important to link up the religious terms we have been discussing with the human experience?

Second Session:

Read "Prelude to Vision" Section (Pages 12-31)

1. How aware do you feel people are to the daily struggles facing humanity?
2. What experience have you had recently that haunts your memory because of its beauty or ugliness. Why? Discuss.
3. Discuss some or all of these examples to determine their relevance to your understanding of Christianity in action.
4. How, specifically, do you see Christ working within these situations?

Third Session:

Read "Day of Love" Section (Pages 32-47)

1. What does the author mean in his line, "Love is all the world has going for it."
2. Discuss the episode of the two boys on Page 41 or the two elderly women on Page 45. In what way was love the bridge in both cases.
3. In what way has your discussion thus far brought out the true meaning of the Eucharist?

Fourth Session:

Read "Day of the Cross" Section (Pages 48-61)

1. When does Christ die?
2. In what sense can we say that the day on which Christ historically died continues to this very day?
3. Discuss the episode in this section that for you most powerfully illustrates Christ dying today.

Fifth Session:

Read "The Day of Fire" Section (Pages 62-81)

1. In what sense can we say the Holy Spirit has the power to re-create the face of the earth?
2. Since He does, why do you think it seems to be happening so slowly?
3. Are there ways that each of us as individuals can help cause this re-creation to take place?

Sixth Session:

Read "Day of All Living" Section (Pages 82-93)

1. Discuss in what way the episode about the girl on Page 84 is a living Easter.
2. In what sense can we say that the Resurrection (or Easter) should be a daily occurence in everyone's daily life?
3. In Jesus' rising from the dead, we rise with Him. Discuss.

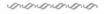

Seventh and Final Session:

1. Discuss the practical meaning of this statement: "The core truth that, in union with Christ, we must pass from death to life."
2. Discuss the concept that by living our daily existence Jesus forever united human experiences with religious terms.
3. Discuss the relevance of numbers 1 and 2 to your own daily living.

Photograph by Charles Nichols

The Author

Reverend Earnest Larsen, C.SS.R., is a compassionate, dynamic and forceful priest dedicated to helping others understand Christ's message as it applies to their lives and life-styles. Father Larsen is nationally known for his writings and for the many workshops, retreats and lectures he conducts around the country. While his efforts are directed to Christians of all ages, he gives special emphasis to the youth of the country, their problems and their Faith. He has the ability of speaking the language of the reader or the listener.

Books already in print: Good Old Plastic Jesus; Don't Just Stand There; Where and How; And Tomorrow We . . .; You Try Love, I'll Try Ajax; Not My Kid; Will Religion Make Sense To Your Child; Will Morality Make Sense To Your Child; Why Don't You Listen; Hey, I Love You, Is That Okay? (Liguorian Publications); Busy Being Born (St. Mary's Press).

Father Larsen was ordained as a Redemptorist priest in 1965 and since that time has served at an inner city parish in St. Louis, a Chicago Retreat House, a parish in Grand Rapids—and currently is working in a parish in Minneapolis where he is deeply involved in Marriage Counselling, Youth Guidance and Religious Education Programs.

His speaking engagements, parish work, involvement as a member of the Chemical Dependence Staff at Anoka State Mental Hospital, and personal commitment to people from all walks of life, reflects in his writings and accounts in part for the "now" approach of his works.